# HALLELUJAH

## The Sound That Heaven Understands

*(Building a Life of Pure Praise)*

***Gerard Assey***

**HALLELUJAH**

**The Sound That Heaven Understands**

***(Building a Life of Pure Praise)***

By

Gerard Assey



*Published by:*

Gerard Assey

19/18, Palli Arasan Street

Anna Nagar East

Chennai - 600 102

**ISBN: 978-81-995134-2-6**

# Table of Contents

# PREFACE

**Why This Book Had to Be Written**

Some words are spoken often, yet understood rarely. "Hallelujah" is one such word.

It is sung across denominations, whispered in prayer, shouted in celebration, and written into countless songs. It rolls easily off our tongues, so familiar that we seldom pause to ask what it truly carries. And yet, in Scripture, this word is anything but casual. It is not decorative language. It is not spiritual punctuation. It is a sound that carries authority, intention, and eternal weight.

This book was born out of a burden rather than a concept—a burden to rescue "Hallelujah" from routine and restore it to revelation.

In many places, worship has become expressive but not always transformative. Praise is abundant, yet power often feels distant. Songs are sung, but heaven sometimes feels silent. This is not because God has withdrawn, but because we have grown accustomed to *using* holy language without fully *understanding* it. Familiarity has dulled wonder. Repetition has replaced revelation.

"Hallelujah" is not merely a word we say—it is a sound heaven recognizes.

Scripture reveals that Hallelujah is spoken in moments of triumph, released in seasons of warfare, offered in valleys of suffering, and echoed endlessly around the throne of God. It is not bound to music, culture, or emotion. It is a command, a confession, a weapon, and a lifestyle. It is spoken before battles are won and after victory is secured. It is uttered by the broken and the redeemed alike.

This book is written for worship leaders who long to move beyond performance into presence. For pastors who desire congregations that do not merely sing, but *align*. For believers who want their praise to carry weight beyond the moment. And for anyone who senses that worship is meant to be more than sound—it is meant to shape life.

You will not find formulas here. You will find revelation. You will not be taught how to sing better, but how to *live louder* in the spirit. You will not be invited to admire Hallelujah, but to *own it*.

Each chapter unfolds one dimension of this sacred word—its origin, its authority, its warfare, its purity, its heavenly pattern, and its generational call. The goal is not information, but transformation. Not admiration, but mandate.

This book asks one central question again and again, in different forms:

Does your Hallelujah sound like heaven—or like habit?

If you read these pages slowly, prayerfully, and honestly, you may discover that Hallelujah is not waiting for your voice alone—it is waiting for your surrender.

Because when Hallelujah is understood, it can no longer remain casual.

And when it is lived, heaven responds.

***Welcome to HALLELUJAH: The Sound That Heaven Understands.***

# INTRODUCTION

## *The Most Spoken Word in Heaven, Yet the Least Understood on Earth*

*"Let everything that has breath praise the Lord. Hallelujah!"* —Psalm 150:6

After this I heard what sounded like the roar of a great multitude in heaven shouting: *"Hallelujah! Salvation and glory and power belong to our God."* —Revelation 19:1

There are many words spoken on earth every day—words of fear, words of ambition, words of despair, words of desire. Yet among all the words that pass human lips, there is one word that heaven never grows tired of hearing. It is a word that does not age, does not weaken, and does not lose its authority with time. That word is *Hallelujah*.

Remarkably, *Hallelujah* is one of the few words that Scripture preserves almost untouched across languages and generations. It is not translated; it is transferred. Whether spoken in Hebrew, Greek, Latin, English, or whispered in a hut or shouted in a cathedral, heaven recognizes it immediately. It is the sound of worship that predates creation and will outlast time itself.

And yet, for all its frequency, *Hallelujah* remains one of the least understood words among believers. It is sung casually, spoken reflexively, and sometimes used emotionally, without revelation. For many, it has become a religious reflex rather than a spiritual declaration. We say it when songs swell, when prayers end, when moments feel right—often without realizing that every time *Hallelujah* is spoken with understanding, something eternal is being released.

This book is written because *Hallelujah* is far more than a musical expression or a verbal punctuation in worship. It is not a filler word while musicians modulate keys or congregations catch their breath. *Hallelujah* is a divine command, a spiritual sound, and an eternal language. It is a word that carries authority in the unseen realm. It is spoken before victory is visible, during warfare when outcomes are uncertain, and after triumph when God's faithfulness stands undeniable.

In the Psalms, *Hallelujah* is often released before circumstances change. David, surrounded by enemies and betrayal, still declared praise to God whom he trusted even when deliverance had not yet arrived. In Psalm 34, written after David escaped from Abimelech, he declared, *"I will bless the Lord at all times; His praise shall continually be in my mouth."* Praise did not wait for safety; it created perspective in danger.

In the Old Testament, praise often preceded power. When King Jehoshaphat faced an enemy alliance too vast to defeat, he did something militarily illogical but spiritually precise. He appointed singers to go ahead of the army, declaring, *"Give thanks to the Lord, for His mercy endures forever"* (2 Chronicles 20:21). Praise was not the celebration of victory—it was the strategy that released it. Though the word *Hallelujah* is not explicitly recorded in that passage, the spirit of it is unmistakable. God responded to praise offered in faith, not fear.

In the New Testament, the language of *Hallelujah* reaches its fullest revelation. In Revelation 19, the apostle John hears heaven erupt with praise as history reaches its climax. "Hallelujah" is shouted not once, but repeatedly—by a great multitude, by the elders, by living creatures. It is the soundtrack of heaven's response to God's justice, salvation, and sovereignty. Heaven does not debate when God acts. Heaven praises.

This alone should arrest us. If *Hallelujah* is the most spoken word in heaven, why is it often the least weighty word on earth?

Part of the reason lies in how worship has subtly shifted over time. In many contexts, worship has become something we *attend* rather than something we *are*. Songs are sung well, musicians are skilled, and lyrics are theologically sound—yet hearts remain discouraged, distracted, or dry. Praise is offered publicly, but privately many believers struggle to sustain worship when the music stops.

Consider a worship leader named Aaron—a gifted musician with a strong voice and deep knowledge of Scripture. On Sundays, he leads the congregation with passion. His hands are lifted, his voice steady, his expressions convincing. People often comment on how powerful the worship feels when he leads. Yet away from the stage, Aaron's inner world tells a different story. He is frequently discouraged, quietly battling disappointment and unanswered prayers. His worship has become professional, but not always personal. He sings *about* God more than he speaks *to* God.

One evening, after a particularly exhausting service, Aaron sat alone in the sanctuary. The lights were off, the instruments silent. In his frustration, he whispered, *"Lord, I don't understand. I sing every week, but I feel empty."* In that stillness, something shifted. Not through a song, not through a sermon—but through revelation. He sensed the Lord gently asking, *"When did your Hallelujah become a performance instead of a proclamation?"*
That question marked the beginning of transformation. Aaron began to realize that *Hallelujah* was never meant to be confined to a melody. It was meant to be a declaration of allegiance, trust, and surrender—spoken not only when surrounded by harmony, but when surrounded by silence. As his understanding grew, his private worship changed before his public ministry did. His Hallelujah became quieter at times, but weightier. And as his heart realigned, his leadership carried a new authority. He was no longer just leading songs; he was releasing heaven.

This book is written for worship leaders like Aaron, for pastors, intercessors, and believers who long for worship that is not shallow or seasonal, but sustaining and transformative. Its purpose is not merely to teach what *Hallelujah* means linguistically, but to restore what it means spiritually.
We will journey together to move *Hallelujah* from habit to holy revelation—so that it is no longer a word we say automatically, but a sound we release intentionally. We will explore how believers can live in praise, release praise in battle, and sustain praise when emotions fluctuate. Above all, this book seeks to train worshippers who do not merely sing songs,

but who understand how to release heaven into earthly spaces.

Because when *Hallelujah* is spoken with understanding, it aligns earth with heaven. It silences the enemy, strengthens the weary, and reminds the soul who God is—regardless of what circumstances say.

The invitation of Scripture is simple, yet profound: *"Let everything that has breath praise the Lord."* Breath is the only qualification. Praise is the response. *Hallelujah* is the sound.

And the question that now stands before us is this: Will *Hallelujah* remain a familiar word on our lips—or will it become a living language in our lives?

This book is an invitation to rediscover that sound.

# CHAPTER 1
## *The Etymology of Eternity: What "Hallelujah" Really Means*

There are some words that belong to a moment, and there are others that belong to eternity. *Hallelujah* is not a word born out of circumstance or culture; it is a word born out of revelation. Long before it was sung by choirs or written into hymnals, it existed as a response of the human spirit to the reality of who God is. To understand *Hallelujah* is to understand not merely a definition, but a posture of the soul.

The psalmist declares, *"Praise the Lord. Praise, O servants of the Lord, praise the name of the Lord! Blessed be the name of the Lord from this time forth and forevermore. From the rising of the sun to its setting, the name of the Lord is to be praised"* (Psalm 113:1–3). These verses do not simply invite praise; they establish its scope. Praise is not seasonal. It is not situational. It is meant to span time, geography, and circumstance. And at the heart of this call to praise lies the word *Hallelujah*.

The word itself is formed from two Hebrew components that carry immense spiritual weight. *Halal* means far more than polite appreciation. It means to boast, to shine, to celebrate extravagantly, even to appear foolish or undignified in expression. It is expressive, visible, and sometimes uncomfortable praise. *Yah* is the shortened form of Yahweh—the self-existent, eternal God who revealed Himself to Moses as "I AM WHO I AM" (Exodus 3:14). This is the God who depends on nothing, is sustained by nothing, and answers to no authority beyond Himself. When these two words come together, *Hallelujah* becomes a command and a confession at once. It is not simply "praise God" in a quiet, internal sense. It literally carries the force of *"let Yahweh be loudly, visibly, unmistakably praised."* It is a summons to bring God out of the shadows of private belief and into the open declaration of public allegiance.

This understanding challenges much of what modern worship has quietly become. Praise, in many settings, has been softened into something restrained, safe, and emotionally controlled. While reverence is essential, Scripture never equates reverence with silence or invisibility. Biblical praise is rarely passive. It moves bodies, lifts voices, and engages the whole person.

**Nowhere is this clearer than in the life of David**.

When the Ark of the Covenant was finally brought back to Jerusalem, David did not respond as a king concerned with image. He responded as a worshipper overwhelmed by the presence of Yah. Scripture tells us that David danced before the Lord *"with all his might"* (2 Samuel 6:14). He removed his royal robes and worshipped with such abandon that his wife Michal despised him in her heart. To her, David had crossed the line of dignity. To God, David had crossed into delight.

David's response to Michal is revealing. He did not apologize for his expression. Instead, he said, *"It was before the Lord… therefore I will celebrate before the Lord. I will become even more undignified than this"* (2 Samuel 6:21–22). David understood something Michal did not: dignity in worship is not defined by human decorum but by divine worth. When Yah is truly seen, *halal* becomes unavoidable.

David's worship was not emotional excess; it was theological accuracy. He had encountered the living God and responded accordingly. His *Hallelujah* was embodied, visible, and unmistakable.

This same revelation runs through the New Testament, though it takes on even deeper clarity through the person of Jesus Christ. In John 17:6, Jesus prays to the Father, saying, *"I have manifested Your name to the people whom You gave Me."* This is a profound statement. In biblical thought, a name is not merely a label—it is a revelation of nature and character. Jesus was saying that through His life, words, and works, He had revealed who the Father truly is.

In other words, Jesus Himself lived *Hallelujah*. His entire earthly ministry was a visible, embodied declaration of the worth of the Father. He glorified God not only through miracles, but through obedience, humility, and surrender—even unto death. Where David danced before the Ark, Jesus became the living Ark, carrying the presence of God among humanity.

When believers say *Hallelujah*, they are not merely echoing a tradition. They are aligning themselves with this long, unbroken revelation—from the God who said "I AM," to the king who danced without shame, to the Son who made the Father known.

Yet many believers struggle here. Praise often becomes passive, restrained by self-consciousness or fear of human opinion.

Consider a believer named Samuel, a quiet man who loved God deeply but rarely expressed it outwardly.

In church, he sang softly, barely moving his lips. His hands remained at his sides, not because he lacked faith, but because he feared appearing foolish. In his mind, worship was something dignified and internal.

One evening, while reading the Psalms alone, Samuel was struck by how physical and expressive biblical worship seemed to be. Words like shout, clap, lift, dance, and rejoice filled the pages. He realized that his hesitation was not rooted in reverence, but in self-awareness. Slowly, intentionally, Samuel began to respond differently in worship. At first, it felt awkward. But over time, as his focus shifted from himself to God, something broke free. His praise became more than sound—it became surrender.

Samuel later reflected that his greatest breakthrough was not emotional; it was revelational. He had redefined dignity. He discovered that true dignity in worship is not about maintaining control, but about yielding it to God.

This is why *Hallelujah* must be intentional. It cannot remain a background word, casually spoken while the heart remains disengaged. Biblical praise is seen, heard, and offered on purpose. It involves the will as much as the emotions. It is a decision to magnify God regardless of mood, moment, or audience.

To remove passivity from praise is to recognize that worship is not something that happens to us; it is something we bring. To redefine dignity in worship is to understand that heaven is not impressed by our composure, but by our sincerity. And to ensure that praise is visible and audible is not about performance—it is about testimony. Praise declares

to the seen and unseen worlds that Yah alone is worthy.
When a believer truly understands what *Hallelujah* means, silence becomes heavier, restraint becomes questionable, and worship becomes personal. The word begins to carry weight again. It is no longer a reflex—it is a revelation.

This chapter invites the reader to pause and ask a simple but searching question: *when I say Hallelujah, am I merely repeating a word, or am I releasing a truth?* Because once *Hallelujah* is understood, it cannot be spoken casually again. It demands the whole heart, the whole voice, and sometimes, the whole body.
And this is only the beginning.

# CHAPTER 2

## *A Command, Not a Suggestion: Hallelujah as a Divine Imperative*

One of the quiet misunderstandings surrounding worship is the assumption that praise is primarily emotional—that it rises naturally when life is good and retreats when life is heavy. While emotions certainly accompany praise, Scripture consistently reveals something deeper and far more demanding. Praise, especially the kind encapsulated in the word *Hallelujah*, is not optional, seasonal, or mood-driven. It is commanded.

The final five psalms—Psalms 146 through 150—form what many scholars call the "Hallelujah Chorus" of the Psalter. Each psalm both begins and ends with the same word: *Hallelujah*. There is no lament here, no petition, no negotiation. The psalmist does not explain circumstances or wait for outcomes. Instead, the command rings out repeatedly, as though heaven itself is insisting that praise must have the final word.

*"Praise the Lord, O my soul,"* the psalmist declares in Psalm 146. This is not an address to a congregation but to the self. The soul is summoned, not consulted. Over and over, the language of these psalms is imperative. Praise God for who He is. Praise Him for what He has done. Praise Him with breath, with instruments, with movement, with sound. And then, as if to leave no room for exception, Psalm 150 concludes, *"Let everything that has breath praise the Lord."*

The striking thing is not just that God commands praise, but *when* He commands it. These psalms were not written in an era of uninterrupted peace. They emerged from a people familiar with exile, warfare, uncertainty, and loss. Praise, therefore, was not prescribed because life was easy, but because praise was essential. God did not command worship because He needed affirmation; He commanded it because His people needed alignment.

**Praise restores what pressure distorts.**
This truth becomes unmistakably clear in the story of Israel at Jericho. When the Israelites finally stood before the fortified city, they were not given siege strategies or battle formations. God's instructions were strange, even unsettling. They were told to march, to remain silent for days, and then, at the appointed moment, to shout. No battering rams. No negotiation. Just obedience expressed through sound.

Joshua 6 records that on the seventh day, when the people lifted their voices as commanded, the walls collapsed. It is important to notice that the shout came *before* the victory was visible. Praise was not the result of triumph; it was the act of trust that preceded it. Israel's Hallelujah was not emotional excitement—it was obedient worship. They praised not because the walls were falling, but because God had spoken.

In every generation, this is the tension believers face. Praise feels natural after breakthroughs, but God calls for praise *before* them. This is where obedience separates mature worship from instinctive response. When praise is commanded, it becomes an act of faith rather than a reflection of feeling.

The New Testament echoes this same imperative, though it often wears quieter clothing. Paul and Silas, imprisoned in Philippi, did not receive an angelic visitation instructing them to sing. They chose to worship because they understood something about praise that transcends comfort. Acts 16 tells us that at midnight, bruised and bound, they prayed and sang hymns to God. Their praise was not strategic—it was instinctive obedience. And once again, praise preceded power. The prison shook. Chains fell. Doors opened.

Praise did not change God's posture toward them; it changed the environment around them and within them.

This is why praise is commanded—not to inform God of our gratitude, but to form us into people who trust Him beyond evidence.

A similar revelation unfolded in a small church led by a pastor named Elias. The congregation had slowly become defined by fatigue. Prayer meetings turned into complaint sessions. Worship felt heavy, and unity was fragile. People loved God, but their language was shaped more by frustration than faith.

One evening, after reading through the Psalms, Pastor Elias sensed a gentle but firm conviction. They had been asking God to fix things, but they had stopped praising Him for who He is. The next few gatherings were intentionally different. Instead of beginning with requests, the church began with deliberate praise—Scripture read aloud, thanksgiving spoken, and worship offered without rushing toward petitions.

At first, it felt unnatural. Some wondered if they were ignoring real problems. But over time, something shifted. Conversations softened. Complaints decreased. Worship grew lighter, not because circumstances had changed, but because hearts had. Unity began to return—not through strategy, but through shared obedience.

What that congregation discovered is what Scripture has always taught: praise recalibrates the soul. When praise is absent, fear grows louder. When praise is restored, perspective follows.

This is why God commands *Hallelujah*. Not because He is insecure, but because He is wise. He knows that what we consistently declare shapes what we eventually believe. Praise realigns us with truth when emotions pull us toward despair.

To live this out requires intentionality. Every believer has areas where praise goes silent—spaces of disappointment, unanswered prayer, or prolonged waiting. These are often the very places God invites praise most strongly. Not as denial, but as declaration. To praise before answers appear is to say, *"God, I trust Your character even when I cannot trace Your hand."*

**Obedient praise does not ignore reality; it confronts it with revelation.**

As this chapter closes, the invitation is simple but demanding. Listen to your own language. Notice where praise has been replaced by resignation or silence. Ask yourself whether your Hallelujah is conditional or commanded. Because the mature worshipper does not wait to feel praise; they choose to obey it.

And when praise becomes obedience rather than emotion, it begins to carry the weight of heaven.
This is the sound God responds to—not because He must, but because obedience always aligns us with His purposes.

# CHAPTER 3
## *Hallelujah in the Valley: Praise That Is Not Circumstance-Dependent*

There is a kind of praise that rises naturally when prayers are answered, when doors open, and when life aligns with expectation. That praise is sincere, and God receives it. But there is another kind of praise—quieter, heavier, and far rarer—that is born not on the mountaintop but in the valley. This is the praise that Scripture holds in highest regard. This is *Hallelujah* spoken not as a reaction to goodness, but as a decision anchored in trust.

The valley is the place where worship is tested. It strips praise of its comfort and exposes its foundation. When circumstances cooperate, praise feels effortless. When they do not, praise becomes intentional. And it is here—when the heart must choose what the mouth will declare—that worship reveals its true nature.

The prophet Habakkuk understood this tension deeply. He lived in a season of national uncertainty, watching injustice flourish and destruction loom. God's answers to his questions were not reassuring in the way he had hoped. Yet instead of retreating into silence, Habakkuk made one of the most courageous declarations in all of Scripture: *"Though the fig tree should not blossom, nor fruit be on the vines… yet I will rejoice in the Lord; I will take joy in the God of my salvation"* (Habakkuk 3:17–18).

Notice the language. Habakkuk does not deny reality. He names the loss plainly—no fruit, no harvest, no visible provision. But he anchors his joy not in what he sees, but in who God is. This is not emotional denial; it is spiritual clarity. His Hallelujah does not wait for restoration. It rises in the absence of it.

This pattern runs consistently through Scripture, nowhere more starkly than in the life of Job. In a single season, Job lost his wealth, his children, his health, and eventually the understanding of those closest to him. His suffering was not the result of sin, nor was it immediately explained. Yet in the raw aftermath of unimaginable loss, Job tore his robe, fell to the ground, and worshiped. His words remain both simple and seismic: *"The Lord gave, and the Lord has taken away; blessed be the name of the Lord"* (Job 1:21).
Job's praise was not polished. It was not sung. It did not come from understanding, but from surrender. Heaven took note of that moment. Job's Hallelujah in pain carried more weight than many praises offered in prosperity, because it declared that God was worthy even when life no longer made sense.

The New Testament mirrors this truth in a scene that is as brutal as it is beautiful. Paul and Silas, having obeyed God's call, found themselves beaten and imprisoned. Their backs were torn, their feet fastened in stocks, their future uncertain. Nothing about their situation suggested victory. And yet Acts 16 tells us that at midnight—at the darkest hour—they prayed and sang hymns to God.

They did not wait until morning. They did not wait until healing came. They did not wait until the chains fell. Their praise rose while they were still bleeding.
This is critical. Their worship did not follow deliverance; it preceded it. And when praise rose from the depths of suffering, the prison shook. Chains fell not because praise is a formula, but because praise aligned heaven's authority with earth's obedience.
This kind of Hallelujah does not ignore pain. It sanctifies it.

For many believers, this is the hardest kind of worship. It is easier to praise when faith feels strong than when the soul feels fragile.
A woman named Miriam learned this in a season she never anticipated. After years of prayer, her marriage ended painfully. The church songs she once sang joyfully now felt distant. Silence seemed more honest than praise.
One evening, sitting alone with her Bible open to the Psalms, Miriam came across words she had read many times but never lived: *"Why are you cast down, O my soul? Hope in God; for I shall again praise Him"* (Psalm 42:11). Something shifted. She realized that Scripture did not shame the downcast soul—it spoke to it. That night, Miriam whispered a simple Hallelujah, not because she felt healed, but because she chose not to let sorrow have the final word.
Her circumstances did not change overnight, but her inner world did. Praise became a lifeline rather than a performance. Over time, Hallelujah became the language she used to remind her own heart that God was still present in the valley.

This is what it means to build a “valley vocabulary” of worship. It is learning to speak praise when emotions argue against it. It is developing the habit of declaring truth when feelings feel unreliable. The valley does not silence praise—it trains it.

A helpful spiritual practice is what might be called a praise audit. Not an exercise of guilt, but of awareness. When was the last time praise came from your lips in the midst of disappointment? Not after resolution, but during waiting. Not after healing, but during weakness. These moments reveal not how loud our worship is, but how rooted it is.

Praise offered in pain carries authority because it testifies that God’s worth is not conditional. It proclaims that He is worthy of worship not only for what He does, but for who He is. This is the Hallelujah heaven recognizes immediately—the sound of trust forged in suffering.

s this chapter draws to a close, the invitation is not to pretend that valleys do not exist, but to refuse to let them redefine God. The valley is not a punishment; it is often a proving ground. And the Hallelujah spoken there is not weaker—it is stronger.

Because when praise rises from the valley, it does not echo—it ascends. And heaven always listens.

# CHAPTER 4
## *When Hallelujah Feels Costly: Worship Across Seasons*

### When Hallelujah Feels Costly: Worship Across Seasons

Every worship leader eventually faces a season when Hallelujah feels heavy, distant, or even impossible. The instruments are ready. The songs are arranged. The people expect joy. Yet the heart feels barren. The silence is deafening. The response of heaven seems delayed.

These seasons are not failures—they are invitations to discover the depth of authentic worship. Scripture repeatedly portrays heroes of faith praising God when it was hard, costly, or uncomfortable. These moments reveal that Hallelujah is not merely a reaction to blessing—it is a declaration of God's worth through every season.

### Worship in Silence: The Weight of Waiting

Consider Ezekiel, who received the most vivid visions of God's glory, yet was commanded to enact strange, silent forms of worship (Ezekiel 24). He was instructed to mourn in the sight of the city, to bind his tongue in certain ways, and to act out God's messages even when no immediate results were visible.

The principle here is clear: God honors worship that persists without immediate reward or confirmation. Silence, waiting, and even apparent inactivity do not negate the power of Hallelujah—they refine it.

**A Real-life Example:**

Naomi, a worship leader in a small coastal church, experienced months where she felt spiritually numb. Every rehearsal felt mechanical. Yet, she committed to pray and sing morning and evening, even when no joy surfaced. Six months later, during a revival service, the worship that had been quietly cultivated in private became the river of life for her congregation. Her faithful Hallelujah in the silence had prepared a spiritual breakthrough.

**Worship in Waiting: The Depth of Patience**

Psalm 130 captures the essence of worship during waiting: *"Out of the depths I cry to You, O Lord. Lord, hear my voice; let Your ears be attentive to my cry for mercy"* (Psalm 130:1–2).

Waiting does not negate worship. It amplifies it. Each prayer, each whispered Hallelujah, stretches the spirit, deepens intimacy with God, and trains the soul to release praise without seeing results immediately.

**Another Example:**

Joshua, a worship pastor, prayed and prepared for a major city-wide outreach. For weeks, attendance was low. Volunteers were discouraged. Yet Joshua chose to lead with a faithful Hallelujah every evening. When the day of the event arrived, not only was the crowd larger than expected, but the worship atmosphere carried a depth that touched hearts profoundly. Waiting had matured the weight of the sound.

**Worship After Failure: Praise in Humility**

Sometimes, Hallelujah must rise after failure. Psalm 51, David's confession after his sin with Bathsheba, is a prime example. Despite guilt, shame, and brokenness, David praises God, offering a contrite heart.

Worship in such seasons is costly, but its authority is undeniable. God is honored when praise rises not despite struggle, but through it.

**A Real-life Illustration:**

Leah, a young worship leader, led a large Sunday service that ended in chaos due to miscommunication among her team. She could have withdrawn in shame, but instead she gathered privately and offered a heartfelt Hallelujah to God, acknowledging His sovereignty and her need for guidance. The next Sunday, the worship carried a new authority—the congregation sensed a deeper, authentic presence of God. Costly worship in seasons of failure resets the spiritual atmosphere.

### Worship in Renewal: Celebration After Restoration

Finally, worship in seasons of renewal is meant to overflow visibly. Nehemiah 12 recounts the dedication of Jerusalem's walls, where priests, Levites, and leaders praised God collectively with instruments, singing, and processions. They had endured seasons of challenge, rebuilding, and waiting—but their worship expressed triumph and gratitude for restoration.

**Another Illustration:**

Caleb, a worship leader who had served in a mission with dwindling attendance, saw the church flourish after years of prayer and obedience. The first service in the renovated sanctuary became a celebration of faithfulness, with Hallelujahs that seemed to carry the echoes of every season prior—dryness, silence, failure, and patience. The sound released was layered with experience, authority, and testimony.

**Practical Revelation for Worship Leaders**

Hallelujah is season-proof. It is the sound that honors God across silence, waiting, failure, and renewal. Understanding this truth empowers leaders to:

- ✓ *Persevere through dry seasons, knowing their praise carries unseen authority.*
- ✓ *Avoid discouragement when emotional or atmospheric responses are minimal.*
- ✓ *Cultivate long-term intimacy and alignment with God that sustains public ministry.*

**Reflection**

Ask yourself:

- ✓ *Am I offering Hallelujah only when it feels easy, or even when it costs me?*
- ✓ *Do I trust that my worship has weight, even if no immediate response is visible?*
- ✓ *Can I celebrate God now, even as I wait for breakthrough or restoration?*

Faithful worship across seasons produces spiritual depth and authority. Leaders who persevere discover that their Hallelujah does not merely echo—they release eternity.

# CHAPTER 5
## *The Sound That Breaks Chains: Hallelujah as a Weapon*

There are moments in Scripture where praise feels gentle—like incense rising quietly before God. And then there are moments where praise sounds like thunder, where worship is not soothing but confrontational. This chapter belongs to the latter. Hallelujah is not only the language of adoration; it is also the sound of warfare. When released with understanding, it does not merely comfort the believer—it unsettles the enemy.

Spiritual battles are rarely won by strength alone. They are won by alignment. Praise aligns the believer with heaven's authority, and that alignment shifts the battlefield. This is why Scripture repeatedly presents praise not after the battle, but at the front of it.

Psalm 149 captures this paradox with striking clarity: *"Let the high praises of God be in their mouths and a double-edged sword in their hands."* Praise and weaponry are not separate images here; they are inseparable realities. The mouth releases what the hand enforces. Praise is not passive—it advances.

Few stories illustrate this more vividly than the account of King Jehoshaphat. When a vast coalition of enemies came against Judah, the situation was humanly impossible. Jehoshaphat's prayer in 2 Chronicles 20 is honest and unembellished: *"We do not know what to do, but our eyes are on You."* God's response did not involve military instruction. Instead, it carried a divine strategy that defied logic: the battle would be won through praise.

Jehoshaphat appointed singers, not soldiers, to go ahead of the army. Their assignment was not to intimidate the enemy, but to exalt God, declaring, *"Give thanks to the Lord, for His mercy endures forever."* As they began to sing, Scripture records something extraordinary. The Lord Himself set ambushes against the enemy forces. Confusion broke out. What Judah could not defeat, God dismantled without their swords ever touching flesh.

The victory was not produced by volume or musical skill. It was released through obedient praise that declared God's character before the outcome was visible. Hallelujah went ahead of the army, and heaven responded by stepping into the battlefield.

This is the essence of praise as a weapon. It does not deny the presence of the enemy; it denies the enemy the final word. Hallelujah confuses the forces of darkness because it announces victory before the battle appears resolved. It speaks from God's perspective, not from human anxiety.

The enemy understands fear, complaint, and despair. Those languages are familiar. Praise, especially praise offered under pressure, disrupts him because it refuses to cooperate with his narrative. When believers praise in the face of threat, they testify that God's authority outweighs visible opposition.

This truth did not remain theoretical for a family named the Thompsons. Over a prolonged season, their household felt relentlessly pressured. Financial strain, health issues, and constant tension filled their conversations. Prayer slowly turned into worry spoken aloud. Even Scripture, when quoted, carried desperation rather than faith.

One evening, exhausted and discouraged, they realized something sobering. Fear had become the loudest voice in their home. Conversations revolved around what might go wrong. Silence felt safer than hope. In that moment of clarity, they made a simple but radical decision. They would change the sound of their house.

They began awkwardly at first. Short prayers of praise at the dinner table. Scriptures spoken aloud in the morning. Worship songs played not for atmosphere, but for declaration. They spoke Hallelujah not because circumstances had changed, but because fear no longer deserved agreement.

Over time, something shifted. Not every problem disappeared immediately, but the heaviness lifted. Peace returned. Unity strengthened. The atmosphere of their home changed because the language changed. Praise became their resistance.

This is how Hallelujah functions as a weapon. It must be spoken, not whispered. Scripture consistently presents praise as audible and declared. Silent admiration has its place, but warfare praise must be voiced. The enemy does not flee from thoughts; he responds to authority released through confession.

Praise is also most powerful when released corporately. There is something about united voices that mirrors heaven's order. When believers praise together, they reinforce one another's faith. This is why so many biblical breakthroughs occur in community settings. Unity amplifies authority.

Finally, praise must be sustained. Sporadic worship may encourage the heart, but consistent praise shapes spiritual posture. The enemy often waits for praise to fade before reasserting pressure. Sustained Hallelujah keeps the ground occupied. It declares that worship is not a tactic—it is a lifestyle.

Chains break not because praise is dramatic, but because it is authoritative. Hallelujah releases truth into contested spaces. It reminds the believer who God is and reminds the enemy where he stands.

As this chapter closes, the question is not whether battles will come—they will. The question is what sound will meet them. Will fear speak first, or will Hallelujah rise before the clash?
Because when praise goes ahead, God steps in behind it. And no chain forged in darkness can withstand the sound heaven has already endorsed.

# CHAPTER 6
## *When Praise Carries Weight: Understanding Spiritual Authority in Sound*

Every worship leader has experienced it.
*Two gatherings.*
*Similar songs.*
*Comparable musicianship.*
*Yet radically different outcomes.*
In one moment, worship feels alive—authoritative, piercing, heaven-aware. The room shifts. Hearts soften. Burdens lift. God feels near, not emotionally, but spiritually tangible. In another moment, everything appears "right," yet the sound feels flat. The songs are sung, but something remains untouched. Heaven feels silent.
This is not coincidence. Scripture reveals a truth that is rarely taught but deeply felt: not all sound carries weight.

The Bible never treats sound as neutral. From the opening words of Genesis to the final Hallelujahs of Revelation, sound precedes movement, shapes reality, and releases authority. But there is a difference between sound that fills space and sound that carries spiritual substance.
In Genesis 1, creation does not begin with action—it begins with voice. *"And God said..."* Light did not emerge because God exerted effort; it appeared because God released sound aligned with His will. Sound preceded manifestation. The authority was

not in volume, but in alignment. God spoke from who He is.

This pattern repeats throughout Scripture. In Ezekiel 37, the valley of dry bones does not respond to observation, emotion, or sympathy. It responds to prophetic sound. When Ezekiel speaks what God commands—not what he feels—bones assemble, breath enters, and life rises. The sound carried weight because it was obedient sound.

This is the first revelation worship leaders must grasp: sound carries authority only when it is aligned with God's will.

Not all sound is spiritual authority. Some sound is emotional release. Emotional release is not wrong—it can be healing—but it is not the same as authoritative praise. Emotional sound flows from how we feel. Authoritative sound flows from who God is. One expresses experience; the other enforces truth.

This distinction explains why heaven responds to some worship and remains silent toward others. Heaven does not respond to musical excellence alone. Heaven responds to alignment.

Psalm 29 describes the voice of the Lord with remarkable language. It calls God's voice *"powerful," "majestic,"* and capable of breaking cedars and shaking wildernesses. The emphasis is not on loudness, but on *weight*. God's voice carries glory because it carries authority. When human worship aligns with God's nature and will, it begins to carry a measure of that same spiritual weight.

This is vividly demonstrated in the story of Jericho. The priests did not shout randomly. They followed precise instruction. The sound that brought walls down was not spontaneous enthusiasm—it was

obedient execution. Trumpets were blown according to divine timing, not emotional impulse. When the shout finally came, it carried accumulated obedience. The walls fell not because Israel was loud, but because Israel was aligned.
In contrast, Scripture also records moments where sound produced no spiritual effect. Israel sang while disobeying. God called it noise. The difference was not sincerity—it was submission. Sound detached from obedience loses weight.

The New Testament reinforces this truth powerfully through Jesus. When Jesus calmed the storm, He did not raise His voice dramatically. He spoke with authority. The wind and waves obeyed because creation recognizes alignment. Jesus' voice carried weight because His will was perfectly aligned with the Father. Authority flowed naturally.
This same principle applies to worship leaders today. Authority in sound does not come from talent, preparation, or passion alone. It flows from obedience. Obedience increases the *density* of worship. It adds spiritual gravity.

**A real-life story illustrates this well.**
Aaron was a gifted worship leader with years of experience. His teams were tight, his arrangements creative, and his services well attended. Yet privately, Aaron sensed something was missing. Worship often stirred emotion, but lasting transformation felt rare. One week, during personal prayer, he felt convicted—not about music, but about unresolved obedience. There were areas of his life he had postponed surrendering.

Aaron made quiet adjustments. He addressed the areas God highlighted. He simplified his approach to worship, focusing less on execution and more on alignment. Over time, something changed. Services became less polished but more potent. Moments of silence carried weight. Short declarations pierced hearts. The sound had not grown louder—but it had grown heavier.

Aaron discovered what Scripture has always taught: obedience gives sound substance.

This is where worship leaders must learn to discern between atmosphere and authority. Atmosphere can be created by sound, lighting, emotion, and arrangement. Authority can only be released by alignment. Atmosphere influences feelings; authority shifts realities.

When worship leaders chase atmosphere without authority, gatherings may feel good but lack staying power. When authority is present, even simple worship reshapes hearts, convicts sin, and invites God's manifest presence.

Heaven does not respond to excellence alone—it responds to agreement. When worship aligns with truth, obedience, and reverence, it begins to carry heaven's weight.

This chapter calls worship leaders to stop asking, *"How did it sound?"* and begin asking, *"Did it carry weight?"*

Because when praise carries weight, chains do not resist. Hearts do not remain neutral. And heaven does not remain silent.

Sound aligned with heaven never returns empty.

# CHAPTER 7
## *Hallelujah and the Throne Room: Joining Heaven's Eternal Song*

There are moments in Scripture where the curtain between earth and heaven seems to part, allowing us to glimpse a reality that exists beyond time and circumstance. In those moments, language falters and imagery stretches the limits of human understanding. Yet one thing remains unmistakably clear: heaven is not silent. Heaven is filled with sound, and at the center of that sound is worship.

When the apostle John was invited into the heavenly realm, he did not encounter debate, strategy, or discussion. He encountered worship. Revelation chapters 4 and 5 do not describe angels holding councils or elders arguing theology. They describe living creatures, elders, and multitudes responding instinctively to the presence of God. Heaven does not reason its way into worship; it responds to revelation. When God is seen clearly, worship is inevitable.

Revelation 4 opens with a throne set in heaven. Everything flows from that throne—authority, judgment, mercy, and glory. The One seated there is not introduced with explanation or defense. God does not justify Himself in heaven. His worth is self-evident. Around Him are living creatures whose sole occupation seems to be declaring, *"Holy, holy, holy is the Lord God Almighty, who was and is and is to come."* Their worship is not repetitive because it is not routine; it is continual because revelation never exhausts itself.

The elders respond by casting their crowns before the throne, acknowledging that everything they are and everything they have originates from Him. This is the first lesson heaven teaches us about worship: when God is rightly seen, self is rightly laid down. Hallelujah begins not with sound, but with surrender.

In Revelation 5, the scene deepens. A scroll appears, sealed and seemingly inaccessible. John weeps, not because he lacks understanding, but because redemption appears delayed. Then the Lamb steps forward—slain, yet standing. When heaven recognizes the Lamb, worship intensifies. A new song erupts, declaring worthiness not based on power alone, but on sacrifice. Heaven worships the Lamb because He was slain. The cross is not an interruption in worship; it is the reason for it.

What is striking is that worship in heaven escalates with revelation. The more God reveals of Himself, the louder and broader the worship becomes. Individuals give way to multitudes. Creatures give way to creation. Eventually, *"every creature in heaven and on earth and under the earth"* joins the song. Worship expands because revelation expands.

This trajectory reaches its climax in Revelation 19, where the word *Hallelujah* appears with a force unmatched anywhere else in Scripture. Four times heaven erupts with Hallelujah, each declaration layered with meaning and authority. This is not casual praise; it is cosmic proclamation.

- ✓ *The first Hallelujah erupts in response to salvation. Heaven recognizes that God's redemptive plan has reached its fulfillment.*

*Salvation is no longer anticipated; it is accomplished.*

- ✓ *The second Hallelujah exalts God's glory, acknowledging that all honor rightly belongs to Him alone.*
- ✓ *The third Hallelujah affirms His honor, declaring His justice as righteous and true.*
- ✓ *The fourth Hallelujah proclaims His power, celebrating that God reigns and His kingdom stands unchallenged.*

These four Hallelujahs are not separate songs; they are a unified declaration of who God is and what He has done. Salvation, glory, honor, and power converge into a single sound. Hallelujah becomes the language that holds all of heaven's theology together.

One of the most profound truths revealed here is this: heaven does not pause to analyze events—it responds in worship. When God acts, heaven answers with Hallelujah. There is no cynicism, no delay, no debate. Worship is immediate because trust is complete.

This stands in sharp contrast to much of earthly worship. On earth, praise is often delayed until understanding arrives. We analyze, question, and sometimes hesitate. Heaven teaches us a different posture. Worship flows not from explanation, but from recognition.

A worship leader named Daniel once struggled deeply with this tension. He loved Scripture and valued sound doctrine, but he often found himself overthinking worship. Services felt heavy, and praise felt restrained. During a season of prayer, he became captivated by the book of Revelation. As he read and reread the throne room scenes, something shifted. He realized that heaven did not wait for perfect conditions to worship. It worshiped because God was worthy—period.

Daniel began to change how he approached worship gatherings. Less emphasis on crafting perfect moments, more emphasis on responding to God's presence. Less explanation, more declaration. Over time, the atmosphere changed. Worship became simpler, yet deeper. People weren't trying to feel something; they were responding to Someone.

This is the alignment heaven invites us into. Earthly worship is meant to echo heavenly patterns. Not replicate them perfectly, but reflect their priorities. Heaven worships God for who He is before celebrating what He does. Heaven worships corporately, without spectators. Heaven worships continually, not episodically.

To join heaven's song is to recalibrate our worship around revelation rather than emotion. It is to allow Hallelujah to rise not only when outcomes please us, but when God reveals Himself to us. This is why worship on earth carries authority when it mirrors heaven. When our Hallelujah aligns with the throne, it carries the resonance of eternity.

A woman named Ruth experienced this alignment during a personal crisis. Facing a long season of uncertainty, she felt disconnected from worship. Songs felt distant, prayers felt mechanical. One night, while reading Revelation 19, she was struck by the sheer decisiveness of heaven's praise. No hesitation. No conditions. Just worship.

She began to practice what she read. Instead of asking God to change her circumstances first, she began declaring who He was. Quiet Hallelujahs filled her prayer time—not emotional, not dramatic, just resolved. Over weeks, her perspective shifted. Peace settled. Not because everything changed, but because her worship had moved closer to the throne.

This is the invitation of this chapter. Hallelujah is not merely a word we speak; it is a sound that aligns us with eternal reality. When we worship, we are not starting something new—we are joining something already in progress. Heaven's song never stops. The question is whether we will harmonize with it.

When earthly worship aligns with heavenly worship, something profound happens. The gap between now and eternity feels thinner. The presence of God feels nearer. Hallelujah becomes more than expression; it becomes participation.

And so the call stands before every believer: lift your Hallelujah not merely toward heaven, but with heaven. Join the song that began before creation and will continue long after history concludes. Because the throne still stands, the Lamb is still worthy, and heaven is still singing.

And that song, above all others, is Hallelujah.

# CHAPTER 8
## *From Lips to Life: When Hallelujah Becomes a Lifestyle*

Most believers learn how to *say* "Hallelujah" long before they learn how to *live* it. The word often finds its way easily onto our lips—in songs, sermons, and spontaneous moments of joy—but struggles to penetrate our schedules, our reactions, our conversations, and our daily decisions. Yet heaven was never interested in borrowed moments of praise alone. God has always desired a people whose entire lives resonate with worship.

Paul captures this longing of God in Romans 12:1 when he urges believers to *"present your bodies as a living sacrifice, holy and acceptable to God, which is your reasonable service."* The language is striking. Worship is no longer confined to an altar, a temple, or even a song. It becomes embodied. It becomes lived. Praise migrates from the mouth to the manner of life. Hallelujah, in its fullest sense, matures when it stops being an occasional expression and becomes a continuous posture.

This is why Colossians 3:17 presses even further: *"Whatever you do, in word or deed, do everything in the name of the Lord Jesus, giving thanks to God the Father through Him."* Notice the breadth of the statement—*whatever you do*. Paul does not carve out sacred and secular categories. Speech and silence, labor and rest, conflict and celebration—all of it is meant to carry the fragrance of gratitude. When thanksgiving saturates action, life itself begins to sound like Hallelujah.

The Old Testament gives us early glimpses of this truth through individuals whose worship extended beyond moments into meaning. Consider Abraham. Scripture does not record him singing many songs, yet his entire journey was marked by obedience that glorified God. In Genesis 22, when Abraham climbs Mount Moriah with Isaac, there is no choir, no congregation, no musical accompaniment. There is only surrender. And yet heaven interprets that obedience as worship. Abraham's Hallelujah was not verbal—it was vocational. His trust proclaimed the worthiness of Yahweh louder than any song could.

David, too, understood this progression. While he is remembered for psalms and instruments, his deepest acts of worship often took place in decision-making moments—refusing to kill Saul, repenting when confronted by Nathan, returning the Ark to its rightful place. David's Hallelujah was not perfect, but it was sincere, woven into repentance, leadership, and dependence. His life oscillated between failure and fervent worship, reminding us that Hallelujah as a lifestyle is not about flawlessness but about orientation.

Jesus Himself models this reality most clearly. Though He often withdrew to pray and worship the Father, His entire earthly life was a continuous offering. Every miracle, every act of compassion, every moment of restraint under accusation was worship in motion. When He washed the disciples' feet in John 13, He transformed a household task into a holy declaration: God is worthy of humble obedience. The cross itself—silent, bloody, obedient—was the loudest Hallelujah heaven ever received from earth. No song accompanied it, yet Revelation tells us that the Lamb who was slain is eternally worshiped because of it.

he early church inherited this understanding. Their praise was not limited to gatherings; it spilled into daily conduct. They worked with integrity, loved across social boundaries, endured persecution without bitterness, and rejoiced even when scattered. Their Hallelujah was audible not only in hymns but in how they lived under pressure. The watching world was not drawn merely by what they sang, but by how they suffered, forgave, shared, and persevered.

A modern illustration may help ground this truth. Consider the story of Samuel Joseph, a familiar figure—a mid-sized business owner navigating relentless pressures. For years, Samuel compartmentalized his faith. Sundays were sacred; weekdays were survival. His prayers were earnest but limited to emergencies. Gratitude appeared only when profits were high and problems were few.

Everything began to change after a season of exhaustion and quiet conviction. Samuel sensed the Spirit nudging him to stop asking God to bless his work and instead start offering his work to God. He began small—thanking God aloud before opening his office each morning, choosing integrity over shortcuts even when it cost him, responding gently rather than sharply to difficult employees, acknowledging God's faithfulness in ordinary moments.

Over time, his workplace atmosphere shifted. Conversations softened. Conflicts resolved faster. Samuel himself changed most of all. Praise no longer waited for breakthroughs; it accompanied spreadsheets, meetings, disappointments, and delays. His Hallelujah no longer depended on outcomes—it flowed from awareness. Work itself became worship.

This is where Hallelujah proves its maturity. It learns to speak not only in sanctuaries but in kitchens, offices, hospital corridors, and long seasons of uncertainty. It learns to honor God in relationships—through patience, forgiveness, restraint, and intentional love. A marriage that chooses kindness over contempt is singing Hallelujah without melody. A parent who prays instead of panics over a prodigal child is releasing worship into the unseen realm.

Perhaps the truest test of a Hallelujah lifestyle is how it behaves in trials. Pain has a way of stripping worship down to its essence. When circumstances refuse to cooperate, praise must decide whether it will retreat or remain. Those who live Hallelujah learn that worship in trials is not denial of reality but declaration of trust. It is not pretending the storm isn't real; it is proclaiming that God is greater than the storm.
This kind of praise does not always sound joyful. Sometimes it is quiet faithfulness. Sometimes it is obedience with tears. Sometimes it is gratitude whispered through clenched teeth. Yet heaven recognizes it. Heaven understands it. Because God is not measuring volume—He is discerning surrender.

When Hallelujah becomes a lifestyle, life itself begins to echo eternity. Worship stops being an event and becomes an atmosphere. The believer no longer asks, *"Is this spiritual?"* but rather, *"Can this glorify God?"* In such a life, praise does not end when the music fades—it continues in footsteps, choices, words, and endurance.

This is the invitation of Hallelujah: not merely to say it, but to *become* it. When lips and life agree, worship becomes credible. And when worship becomes a way of life, heaven hears a sound it understands well—the sound of a life wholly offered to God.

# CHAPTER 9

## *Before the Microphone: The Hidden Altar of the Worshipper*

There is a sound that fills sanctuaries but never reaches heaven. And there is a sound that rises quietly from unseen places and moves the heart of God. The difference is not volume, skill, or sincerity in the moment—it is the condition of the altar on which the sound is born.

Long before Hallelujah becomes a public declaration, it is first a private decision.
Scripture repeatedly reveals a pattern that modern worship culture often resists: God listens carefully to *who* is speaking before He responds to *what* is being sung. Public Hallelujah may inspire people, but private obedience is what gives that Hallelujah spiritual weight.

David understood this long before he stood before armies or ascended thrones. The same David who declared, *"I will bless the Lord at all times; His praise shall continually be in my mouth"* (Psalm 34:1), was first a shepherd whose songs were heard by God alone. His authority before Goliath was not rooted in confidence—it was rooted in history. David did not meet God on the battlefield; he met Him in fields where no applause followed his worship.
When David stood before Goliath, he carried no instrument, sang no melody, and lifted no chorus. Yet heaven responded instantly. Why? Because the sound of his life already aligned with the sound of his

confession. David had already learned how to say Hallelujah when nobody was listening.
This principle confronts a dangerous illusion: that public worship can compensate for private compromise. It cannot.

Isaiah speaks with sobering clarity when he records the Lord's complaint: *"These people draw near with their mouths and honor Me with their lips, but their hearts are far from Me"* (Isaiah 29:13). God was not rejecting their songs; He was rejecting the distance between their sound and their surrender.

A worship leader may be skilled and sincere, yet still spiritually dull if the private altar has been neglected. Compromise rarely silences worship immediately—it dulls sensitivity first. The songs continue, the hands lift, the crowd responds—but heaven grows quiet.
This is why Jesus, though constantly surrounded by need, noise, and opportunity, repeatedly withdrew to lonely places to pray (Luke 5:16). His authority in public flowed directly from intimacy in private. Every command that calmed storms and cast out demons was first shaped in solitude. Jesus never treated public ministry as a substitute for private communion.

The Levites understood this long before microphones existed. Before they ministered before the people, they were consecrated before God. Their garments, bodies, and hearts were set apart. The altar came before the assembly. Their service was not entertainment—it was stewardship of sacred sound.

Consider the story of Eliab Matthews, a familiar figure in many churches. Eliab was a gifted worship leader, widely admired for his musical excellence and spiritual vocabulary. His songs moved people deeply, yet privately, his prayer life had become rushed, his repentance delayed, and his obedience selective. Over time, he noticed something troubling. The moments that once carried authority began to feel hollow. The crowd still applauded, but the room no longer shifted.

It was not until Eliab stepped away from the stage for a season—returning to Scripture without instruments, to prayer without performance—that his sensitivity was restored. He later testified that his most powerful Hallelujahs were born not during rehearsals, but during quiet mornings of repentance and realignment. The microphone had amplified his voice, but the altar had restored his authority.

Applause is not the enemy—but it is a dangerous substitute for affirmation from God. The greatest threat to a worship leader's intimacy is not failure, but familiarity. When sacred moments become routine, reverence quietly leaks away. Hallelujah turns automatic instead of intentional.

The psalmist warns, *"If I regard iniquity in my heart, the Lord will not hear me"* (Psalm 66:18). This is not a statement of condemnation, but of alignment. God is not silenced by weakness—He is resisted by willful disconnect.

A worship leader must therefore guard tenderness more fiercely than gifting. Gifting opens doors; tenderness keeps heaven open. It is possible to sing about surrender while quietly protecting areas God is asking to touch. Over time, that resistance alters the sound.

There is a difference between singing *to* God and standing *before* Him.

Another example is that of Miriam Jojo, a young worship leader whose private discipline shaped her public authority. Long before she led congregations, she learned to turn ordinary moments into altars—washing dishes while praying, driving in silence with Scripture, fasting not for visibility but for sensitivity. When she eventually stood on a platform, her Hallelujah carried a gravity that could not be rehearsed. People often said, *"There's something different when she leads,"* but what they felt was not talent—it was consecration.

This is the hidden truth every worship leader must confront: the platform reveals what the altar has produced. Sound does not create authority—it exposes it.

Before the microphone, there must be a place where no one sees, no one hears, and no one applauds—except God. That place is where Hallelujah matures from a word into a way of life.

Public worship may move atmospheres, but private obedience moves heaven.

And when a worship leader learns to say Hallelujah in secret—when praise becomes a lifestyle rather than a setlist—then every public sound carries eternity within it.

The most powerful Hallelujah is not the one sung the loudest. It is the one that costs the most in private. That is the hidden altar. And heaven never ignores it.

# CHAPTER 10
## *Discerning the Sound You Are Releasing*

**Discerning the Sound You Are Releasing**
Every worship leader eventually confronts a moment of silence in the spirit—a moment when the music, the voices, the arrangements are perfect, yet something essential seems absent. The people respond. The applause comes. But heaven does not seem to respond in the same measure. Why?
This is the moment where discernment is required. The revelation of Hallelujah is not merely in singing, shouting, or playing—it is in releasing the sound that carries heaven's weight. And to release such a sound, a worship leader must first discern what they are releasing.

The Old Testament gives us guidance. Consider the priests of Jericho (Joshua 6). They blew the trumpets in obedience, following precise instructions. The people shouted as commanded, not as the heart dictated. The walls fell. Obedience defined authority. The sound carried heaven's weight because it was aligned with God's plan, not merely human intention. Conversely, we see Israel offering worship without alignment, and God calls it noise (Isaiah 29:13).

The New Testament continues the pattern. When Jesus calmed the storm, He did not raise His voice in desperation. He spoke with authority. The waves obeyed. Authority in sound flows from alignment with

God's will, not from volume, technical skill, or audience reaction.

For modern worship leaders, this is a profound challenge: we often conflate emotional engagement, crowd response, or musical excellence with spiritual authority. But heaven measures by different criteria.

To help leaders navigate this, let us enter the realm of reflection—not condemnation. Consider the life of Eliora, a worship pastor. Eliora led large congregations and frequently moved people to tears. But she sensed fatigue in her own spirit. Her worship felt mechanical at times. In her private devotional life, she realized that some songs were led to meet expectations or evoke applause rather than release authentic praise. Once she acknowledged this, she shifted her focus. She began evaluating each rehearsal, each song set, not for performance value, but for spiritual resonance. Within months, the atmosphere changed. Worship now moved from a series of beautiful moments to a series of Spirit-led encounters.

This is the essence of discerning the sound you release: asking, *"Is this worship responding to God, or merely reacting to people?"*

Worship leaders often face another subtle trap: mistaking activity for authority. Leading songs is not the same as stewarding sound. Creating musical moments is not the same as cultivating spiritual movements. The difference lies in intentionality and alignment. When a leader sings from routine, instinct, or habit, they produce applause. When a leader sings from alignment, they release heaven.

Consider David before the Lord (1 Samuel 16). David's harp did not simply soothe Saul; it aligned with God's Spirit. The music carried authority because David had spent years cultivating intimacy with God, listening to His voice, and stewarding his gifts in obedience. The sound he released was not accidental—it was deliberate and Spirit-infused.

Another example comes from Miriam, a worship leader who consistently led spontaneous "Hallelujah" moments in youth gatherings. Miriam noticed that some nights, despite excellent music, hearts remained closed. On other nights, simple chords and soft singing produced breakthroughs. Through reflection, she discerned that her personal alignment, attitude, and focus determined whether heaven responded. The crowd alone never dictated the result.

Discerning your sound requires courage to self-reflect:

- ✓ *Are our words, songs, and declarations originating from obedience or expectation?*
- ✓ *Are we cultivating spiritual movements, or merely curating musical moments?*
- ✓ *Are we mindful that every note, lyric, and gesture releases authority—or emptiness?*

This is not a call to guilt, but to stewardship. The same voice that can release chains can also produce noise that empties the room spiritually. The difference is discernment.

Psalm 33:3 instructs: *"Sing to Him a new song; play skillfully with a shout of joy."* Notice the sequence: a new song—a deliberate act. Skillful play—a prepared instrument. Shout of joy—a heart aligned in freedom and obedience. Worship leaders must evaluate each layer of sound through the lens of spiritual alignment.

As worship leaders, our role is sacred: to steward sound that moves heaven. The measure is not applause, trends, or technical precision. It is alignment, intention, and obedience. When sound is discerned, every note, every declaration, every Hallelujah becomes a conduit of heaven to earth.

Eliab, another example to consider, led a large church team and often felt pressured to "create moments." Over time, he implemented a nightly reflection practice with his team. Before every rehearsal, they paused to evaluate their hearts. They asked: *"Is this worship for God or for people? Are we aligned, or are we distracted? Are we releasing authority or just creating atmosphere?"* That simple practice transformed their worship ministry. Moments that once felt routine now carried weight. Heaven responded.

The reality is clear: Hallelujah is not casual. Sound is not neutral. Every act of worship either carries authority or it does not.

This chapter is an invitation to pause, reflect, and recalibrate. It is an encouragement to every worship leader: before you sing, before you play, before you lead—discern the sound you are releasing. Heaven will respond to alignment, obedience, and stewardship. The crowd may applaud regardless, but only heaven can confirm the authority of your Hallelujah.

**Closing Reflection/Prayer:**

*"Lord, help me to steward the sound I release. Let every note, every lyric, and every Hallelujah come from a heart aligned with You. Remove the desire for applause and increase my sensitivity to Your Spirit. May my sound carry Your authority, not mine. Amen."*

# CHAPTER 11

## *Corporate Hallelujah: The Power of United Praise*

There is a kind of praise that rises from private devotion, and there is another kind that can only be born in community. Personal Hallelujah carries intimacy, but corporate Hallelujah carries authority. When one voice praises, heaven listens; when many voices praise as one, atmospheres respond. Scripture consistently reveals that God does something unique when His people worship Him together in unity—something that does not happen in isolation.

Psalm 133 opens with a declaration that feels almost astonished in tone: *"Behold, how good and how pleasant it is when brothers dwell in unity!"* The psalmist is not merely celebrating relational harmony; he is unveiling a spiritual principle. Unity is not only pleasant—it is powerful. David goes on to compare it to sacred oil poured on Aaron's head, flowing down his beard and garments, and to the dew of Hermon descending on Mount Zion. Both images point to abundance, consecration, and life. Unity creates conditions where God commands blessing. Praise offered in unity becomes a conduit through which heaven releases what earth cannot manufacture.

Corporate Hallelujah is not simply many people singing at the same time. It is alignment of hearts, intention, and focus. When unity converges with praise, worship becomes more than expression—it becomes proclamation. Heaven recognizes it as agreement. Hell recognizes it as threat.

The Old Testament offers a striking picture of this during the dedication of Solomon's Temple. In 2 Chronicles 5, the priests bring the Ark of the Covenant into its place, and the musicians—Levites with cymbals, harps, and lyres—stand together east of the altar. Scripture emphasizes that *"the trumpeters and singers were as one, to make one sound to be heard in praising and thanking the Lord."* That phrase is intentional. They were not merely synchronized musically; they were unified spiritually. When they lifted their voices, declaring, *"For He is good, for His mercy endures forever,"* something extraordinary happened. The house of the Lord was filled with a cloud—the glory of God so tangible that the priests could not stand to minister.
Notice the order. The glory did not descend because the building was magnificent, nor because the sacrifices were many, nor because Solomon's prayer was eloquent—though all of those were present. The glory fell when praise became unified. When many voices carried one confession, God manifested His presence in a way that overwhelmed human activity. Corporate Hallelujah made room for divine interruption.

This same principle reappears in the New Testament, particularly in Acts 2. The early believers were not merely waiting for power; they were waiting together. Luke is careful to say they were *"all with one accord in one place."* Unity preceded outpouring. When the Holy Spirit descended, it was not upon a scattered group of individuals but upon a gathered

body. And when they began to speak, the sound that emerged was not chaotic noise but heaven-inspired utterance. The church was born in an atmosphere saturated with united praise and expectancy.
Later in Acts, we see how this unity expressed itself beyond the upper room. Believers continued *"daily with one accord,"* breaking bread, praying, praising God, and enjoying favor with all the people. Their corporate Hallelujah was not confined to worship services; it shaped communal life. As a result, Scripture tells us the Lord added to the church daily. Growth followed unity. Influence followed praise.

What happens in the spiritual realm when corporate Hallelujah rises? Atmospheres shift. Spiritual resistance weakens. Fear loses its grip. Faith becomes contagious. Praise multiplied by unity does not add—it multiplies. One burning coal warms a space; many coals together ignite a fire.

A realistic example helps illustrate this. Consider a congregation called Rivergate Fellowship, led by a weary but sincere pastor named Daniel Matthews. Over time, the church had become fragmented. Worship services were technically sound, but spiritually thin. People sang, yet their hearts were distracted. Some evaluated music styles, others compared worship leaders, and a quiet consumer mindset settled in. Praise existed, but unity did not.
After a season of prayer and honest conversation, Pastor Daniel realized the issue was not song selection—it was sound alignment. He began teaching the congregation what praise truly was, not as performance but as participation. He spoke openly about worship as agreement with God rather than

enjoyment of music. Slowly, intentionally, the culture began to change. Before songs were sung, Scripture was read. Before melodies were lifted, hearts were invited to align. People were encouraged not merely to sing louder, but to sing together—with awareness, intention, and reverence.

Something shifted. Conversations changed. Complaints diminished. Intercession deepened. During one particular gathering, without any dramatic prompting, the congregation lifted a simple Hallelujah together—not shouted, not forced, but unified. Many later testified that the atmosphere felt "different," heavier yet peaceful. Longstanding tensions eased. A spirit of joy returned. Corporate Hallelujah did what sermons alone could not.

This is why worship leadership is less about managing music and more about stewarding sound. Sound is spiritual. Scripture repeatedly affirms that what is released vocally carries weight in unseen realms. Worship leaders, therefore, are not merely musicians; they are gatekeepers of atmosphere. Their task is not to impress heaven with skill, but to align earth with heaven's sound.

Teaching congregations to praise intentionally becomes essential. People must understand that worship is not a warm-up to preaching; it is ministry in itself. When believers realize that their voices contribute to a collective offering, participation deepens. Unity strengthens. Praise matures.

Moving beyond song selection requires discernment. A song may be beautifully written yet unsuitable for a moment. Heaven is not moved by trend but by truth. Sound stewardship involves asking not only, *"Is this song popular?"* but *"Does this sound align with what God is doing among us now?"* When worship leaders listen to the Spirit and shepherd the congregation into agreement, corporate Hallelujah becomes a holy force rather than a routine.

Ultimately, united praise is a foretaste of eternity. Revelation paints a picture of a great multitude from every nation, tribe, people, and language, crying out with one voice before the throne. Heaven is not divided. Heaven does not compete. Heaven worships in harmony. Every time the church on earth praises in unity, it rehearses for that eternal reality.

Corporate Hallelujah reminds us that we were never meant to worship alone. Our voices were designed to blend, our hearts to align, our praise to converge. And when it does, heaven listens attentively—because it recognizes the sound.

# CHAPTER 12

## *Hallelujah and Thanksgiving: The Gateway to God's Presence*

Many believers long for deeper encounters with God yet struggle to sustain them. They touch moments of intensity in worship, only to feel distant again days later. Scripture reveals a simple but often neglected truth: praise may ignite the fire, but thanksgiving keeps it burning. Hallelujah opens the heavens, but thanksgiving stabilizes the heart. Without gratitude, praise becomes occasional. With thanksgiving, worship becomes a pathway that leads steadily into God's presence.

Psalm 100 is not poetic suggestion; it is divine instruction. *"Enter His gates with thanksgiving, and His courts with praise."* The psalmist does not reverse the order. Thanksgiving is the entrance, praise is the progression, and the presence of God is the destination. Many attempt to leap directly into deep worship without passing through the gate, and when they do, their worship feels forced or fleeting. God, in His wisdom, designed thanksgiving as the posture that prepares the soul for encounter.

Thanksgiving acknowledges what God has done. Hallelujah declares who He is. When gratitude anchors the heart, praise flows with clarity and confidence. This is why Scripture repeatedly links thanksgiving with enduring worship. Psalm 106:1 declares, *"Praise the Lord. Give thanks to the Lord, for He is good; for His mercy endures forever."* Here, praise and thanks are intertwined, yet thanksgiving grounds the declaration of mercy in remembrance. The soul that remembers remains steady.

The Old Testament is filled with examples of thanksgiving functioning as a gateway to God's presence. One of the clearest appears in the life of David. Before David was king, before the Ark was restored to Jerusalem, he cultivated a heart of gratitude in obscurity. The psalms reveal a man who constantly rehearsed God's faithfulness—deliverance from lions, protection from Saul, mercy in failure. David's Hallelujah was never disconnected from thanksgiving. He praised God not only for what was coming, but for what had already been carried through. This is why David could worship even while hunted. Gratitude kept his praise alive when circumstances were hostile.

In the New Testament, Jesus Himself highlights the power of thanksgiving through the account of the ten lepers in Luke 17. All ten were healed. Only one returned. And it was not merely healing that Jesus acknowledged—it was gratitude. *"Were there not ten cleansed? But where are the nine?"* The one who returned did not just receive physical restoration; he encountered the Healer personally. Thanksgiving distinguished him. Gratitude moved him from miracle to relationship. This pattern remains true. Many receive answers, but few enter deeper communion because they move on without returning in thanks.
Thanksgiving sustains what praise initiates because it trains the heart to recognize God's hand in every season. Praise can erupt in moments of victory, but thanksgiving must be practiced daily. It is not dependent on emotion; it is cultivated through

intention. This cultivation changes the internal atmosphere of the believer, often before any external change occurs.

Consider the story of Miriam Thomas, a committed believer who quietly battled chronic anxiety for years. Her prayers were sincere, her worship emotional, yet her mind rarely rested. She praised God in church but lived the rest of the week mentally exhausted by *"what ifs."* One day, during a simple devotional reading of Psalm 100, something unsettled her—in a good way. She realized she was constantly asking God for peace but rarely thanking Him for the peace He had already given in small measures.

Miriam made a deliberate decision to shift her approach. Each morning, before presenting requests, she began listing reasons to thank God—specific, ordinary, sometimes unimpressive reasons. She thanked Him for sleep, for breath, for a steady job, for moments of calm she had overlooked. At first, it felt mechanical. But over time, gratitude softened her inner tension. Her prayers became less frantic. Praise flowed more naturally. Anxiety did not vanish overnight, but its grip weakened. Thanksgiving rewired her focus. By the time she entered praise, her heart was already at rest.

This is how thanksgiving works. It reorients the soul from lack to provision, from fear to faithfulness. When believers begin with thanks, they resist the urge to use worship as an emotional escape. Instead, worship becomes a response to truth remembered. Praise then rises not as effort but as overflow.

As thanksgiving matures into praise, the believer moves deeper into worship—beyond words, beyond structure, into awareness of God's nearness. This progression is not ritualistic; it is relational. Thanksgiving acknowledges God's acts. Praise exalts His nature. Worship surrenders to His presence. Skipping thanksgiving often results in shallow worship because the heart has not been aligned.

The tabernacle pattern in the Old Testament subtly reinforces this movement. Entry required acknowledgement of sacrifice. Progression required praise. The Holy Place and Most Holy Place demanded reverence and surrender. God has always guided His people inward step by step. Thanksgiving is the step that prevents worship from becoming self-focused.

Hallelujah, when rooted in thanksgiving, becomes resilient. It does not fade when emotions fluctuate. It does not collapse under delay. Gratitude steadies praise so that worship becomes a dwelling place rather than a momentary visit.

As this chapter closes, the invitation is simple but transformative: return to thanksgiving. Not as obligation, but as access. Every genuine encounter with God begins at the gate. And the gate has a name—gratitude.

# CHAPTER 13
## *Misunderstood Praise: What Hallelujah Is NOT*

One of the greatest dangers in spiritual life is familiarity without understanding. Few words suffer from this more than "Hallelujah." It is spoken often, sung loudly, and written frequently, yet it can easily drift from revelation into routine. When that happens, praise remains audible but loses authority. Heaven hears sound, but responds to substance.

Scripture never condemns praise itself; it confronts the heart behind it. God is not offended by volume, but He is unmoved by emptiness. This chapter is not about reducing worship, but about restoring its weight. To understand what Hallelujah truly is, we must first confront what it is not.

Isaiah delivers one of the most sobering assessments of worship in all of Scripture: *"These people draw near to Me with their mouth and honor Me with their lips, but their heart is far from Me."* The tragedy here is not silence—it is activity without alignment. God acknowledges that words are spoken, but He exposes the distance of the heart. Hallelujah, when detached from obedience, becomes noise rather than offering. Sound without submission may fill a room, but it does not move heaven.

Throughout the Old Testament, Israel learned this lesson painfully. They mastered the mechanics of worship while neglecting the posture of surrender.

Amos captures God's grief with startling clarity when the Lord declares, "*Take away from Me the noise of your songs; for I will not hear the melody of your stringed instruments.*" God does not reject music; He rejects contradiction. When praise contradicts lifestyle, worship becomes offensive rather than fragrant.

True Hallelujah cannot coexist with persistent disobedience. This does not mean perfection is required, but repentance is essential. Praise is never a substitute for obedience; it is meant to flow from it. Saul learned this when Samuel confronted him, saying, *"To obey is better than sacrifice."* Saul offered worship while withholding surrender, and God exposed the hollowness of it. Hallelujah cannot cover rebellion. It can only crown obedience.

Another distortion of Hallelujah is routine without reverence. When praise becomes habitual rather than intentional, it loses its sharpness. Routine can keep worship consistent, but reverence keeps it alive. Without reverence, words are repeated while awareness fades. Jesus addressed this in His own generation, confronting religious leaders who were fluent in prayer but absent in awe. Their worship was polished, but their hearts were unmoved.

In the New Testament, Jesus' cleansing of the temple was not a rejection of worship, but a protest against misuse. The temple had become busy but barren, active but unholy. Worship had turned transactional. This moment reminds us that God is not impressed by repetition. He responds to reverence. Hallelujah spoken without consciousness

of God's holiness becomes casual speech rather than sacred declaration.
There is also a form of misunderstood praise that substitutes singing for surrender. Songs are powerful, but they are not synonymous with worship. Worship begins where the will yields. The rich young ruler in the Gospels had moral discipline and religious respectability, but when Jesus invited surrender, he walked away sorrowful. Had he sung, his voice would have carried, but his life was unwilling. Hallelujah that does not translate into yielded living remains incomplete.
This tension appears clearly in Romans 12:1, where Paul urges believers to present their bodies as living sacrifices. He calls this *"true and proper worship."* Worship, then, is not confined to sound—it is expressed through surrender. Hallelujah that rises from lips but resists lordship is fragmented praise.

A beautiful story illustrates this quietly but powerfully. Jonathan was a gifted worship musician, deeply admired for his ability to lead songs that moved congregations emotionally. Yet offstage, his life was marked by unresolved bitterness and unrepentant compromise. He told himself that God understood his struggles, and he continued leading worship week after week. Over time, his joy faded. His songs remained strong, but his spirit grew weary.
One evening, after leading a powerful set, Jonathan felt unexpectedly empty. It was not exhaustion; it was conviction. He realized that his Hallelujah had become automatic—muscle memory rather than heart response. In private prayer, he stopped singing and started surrendering. Repentance preceded restoration. When his life realigned, his worship

regained weight. The sound did not change dramatically, but the authority did.
This is the heart check every believer must face. Is my Hallelujah authentic, or is it automatic? Does it flow from reverence, or from routine? Is it supported by obedience, or contradicted by compromise?

God is not seeking flawless worshippers, but truthful ones. He is drawn to honesty more than harmony. Hallelujah does not need to be loud to be powerful, but it must be real. Heaven does not echo empty sound; it responds to surrendered hearts.

As this chapter closes, the invitation is not to sing less, but to mean more. To allow Hallelujah to be purified—not silenced. Because when praise is aligned with obedience, reverence, and surrender, it ceases to be misunderstood. It becomes what it was always meant to be: a sound heaven recognizes and responds to.

# CHAPTER 14
## *Let Everything That Has Breath: A Global, Generational Call*

The final verse of Psalm 150 does not whisper. It does not explain itself gently or invite debate. It thunders with simplicity and finality: "Let everything that has breath praise the Lord. Hallelujah!" This is not merely the conclusion of a psalm; it is the climax of Scripture's worship narrative. After centuries of history, prophecy, lament, deliverance, failure, and restoration, the Bible ends the Psalms the way heaven lives—calling all that breathes to praise.

Praise, according to Scripture, is not reserved for the gifted, the trained, or the positioned. It is the responsibility of the living. Breath itself becomes the qualification. If God has sustained life, then life owes Him Hallelujah. This command dissolves spiritual elitism. Worship is not the domain of the platform; it belongs to every breathing soul.

Creation understands this instinctively. Psalm 19 declares that the heavens speak, even without words. Mountains do not debate whether God is worthy. Oceans do not weigh circumstances before roaring. Trees clap without instruction. Yet humanity, uniquely gifted with will and reason, must choose to praise. Romans 8:19 reveals something striking: creation waits, groans even, for the revealing of the sons of God. Nature praises by design; humanity praises by decision. And heaven waits for that decision.

The tragedy is not that humans cannot praise—it is that they often delay it. We postpone worship until conditions improve, until prayers are answered, until life stabilizes. Creation does not wait. It responds to the Creator by existing as intended. When humans finally choose praise, they align with the rhythm creation has never left.

Throughout the Old Testament, God repeatedly re-centered worship away from select individuals and toward generational inheritance. Altars were not built for moments; they were raised for memory. Abraham built altars not as performance, but as testimony. Isaac and Jacob returned to them, not because they were impressive, but because they marked encounters. An altar outlives a song. A stage fades; an altar speaks.

Solomon's dedication of the temple illustrates this generational scope of worship. When the priests and musicians lifted their voices together, Scripture records that the glory of the Lord filled the house so powerfully that they could not stand to minister. This was not performance; it was alignment. Worshipers were not showcasing skill; they were stewarding sound. Their Hallelujah created space for God's presence to rest among generations.

The New Testament carries this vision forward. At Pentecost, praise was not limited to one voice or one age group. The Spirit fell on sons and daughters, young and old. Worship erupted not from a stage, but from surrendered hearts. The early church was not built on performance culture, but on shared devotion. Their praise carried power because it carried ownership. Everyone participated.

A familiar story illustrates this contrast. Daniel was a talented worship leader in a growing urban church. Services were well-produced, transitions seamless, and attendance strong. Yet something troubled him. Outside of Sunday mornings, few people sang. Worship belonged to the platform, not the people. Children watched, youth observed, adults consumed. Daniel made a quiet shift. He began teaching the theology of praise, not just rehearsing songs. He encouraged families to worship at home, even imperfectly. He invited children into moments of prayer, not as spectators but as participants. Over time, the sound of the church changed. Not louder—deeper. Hallelujah rose from the congregation with ownership, not imitation. Worship became generational.
This is the call of Psalm 150. Not to raise better singers, but truer worshippers. Not to build stages that impress, but altars that endure. Performers seek applause; worshippers seek presence. Performers ask, *"How did it sound?"* Worshippers ask, *"Did God dwell among us?"*

The vision of Hallelujah is global, but it is also deeply personal. Every generation must answer the call anew. Worship cannot be inherited; it must be chosen. Parents can model it, leaders can teach it, but each heart must decide. When one generation fails to pass on worship as revelation, the next inherits it as routine.

This chapter ends not with instruction, but with invitation. To breathe is to qualify. To live is to be summoned. Hallelujah is not reserved for church gatherings or musical moments—it is the rightful response of all creation, and especially of those redeemed.

Let everything that has breath praise the Lord. Not someday. Not selectively. Not performatively. But fully, freely, and faithfully. Because when humanity finally joins creation in unreserved praise, heaven does not need to explain itself—it responds.

# CHAPTER 15
## *Hallelujah and the Next Generation: Raising Voices for Eternity*

**Hallelujah and the Next Generation: Raising Voices for Eternity**

Worship is not merely a present experience; it is a conveyor of legacy. Every Hallelujah offered today has the potential to shape tomorrow. Yet too often, leaders focus only on performance, crowd response, or musical excellence. What if we began to see worship as formation rather than entertainment—an intentional act of raising disciples who will release Hallelujah long after we are gone?

**Teaching Children to Praise Before Performance**

From the earliest days of Israel, worship was taught to the young. David, though a shepherd boy, learned to lift his voice and play the harp before leading armies in praise. The Levites were trained from childhood in music, instruments, and song (1 Chronicles 15:16–22). They were not taught for applause—they were taught for alignment, for the service of God.

**A Real-life Example:**

Hannah, a worship leader in a mid-sized church, noticed that children in her ministry could recite songs perfectly but had no sense of God's presence. She instituted a simple practice: before teaching them tunes, she began each session with a brief story from Scripture and a time of guided, heartfelt praise, emphasizing that their voices were for God, not the teacher or audience. Over months, the children began to sing with joy, reverence, and understanding, even spontaneously during church services. Hallelujah became a declaration, not a performance.

This principle reminds us that training the next generation is not about notes or technique, but about forming hearts to praise God authentically.

**Worship as Formation, Not Entertainment**

Too often, worship is reduced to a stage performance. Children mimic movements, memorize words, and focus on applause. Yet the purpose of Hallelujah is far deeper. It forms character, instills faith, and creates spiritual sensitivity.

**OT Example:**

Josiah, king of Judah as a boy, inherited worship in a temple filled with neglect. Guided by his tutors and mentors, he learned to fear God and praise Him even in the midst of corruption (2 Kings 22). By nurturing him early, God prepared a leader whose worship and obedience reshaped a nation.

**NT Example:**

Paul instructed Timothy, who had been taught the Scriptures from childhood (2 Timothy 3:14–15), to continue in faith and sound teaching. Worship and spiritual formation in youth became the foundation for ministry that impacted generations.

**A Real-life Illustration:**

Micah, a worship pastor, led weekly children's worship sessions where the focus was on thanksgiving, repentance, and personal connection to God. He emphasized that singing is not about entertaining adults or peers, but about training the heart to respond to God in every circumstance. Over the years, many of these children became worship leaders themselves, carrying the same revelation.

### Passing Revelation, Not Just Songs

Songs are tools; revelation is the treasure. A child can memorize twenty songs without understanding why they praise, but when a child experiences the reality of God's presence, that worship becomes lifelong.

Psalm 78:4–7 highlights this principle: *"We will not hide them from their children; we will tell the next generation the praiseworthy deeds of the Lord, His power, and the wonders He has done…so that they might set their hope in God and not forget His works."*

**A Real-life Example:**

Eliana, a worship leader in a rural community, began including small testimonies in her children's choir rehearsals—stories of God's faithfulness, answered prayers, and provision. The children did not only learn the songs; they internalized the narrative of God's greatness, and their Hallelujahs became informed and powerful. Parents began noticing changes—children prayed spontaneously, praised at home, and shared faith stories with siblings.

The principle is clear: passing revelation shapes generations, while passing only songs produces temporary sound. A true Hallelujah ministry invests in eternal impact.

### Practical Insights for Worship Leaders

Raising a generation of authentic worshippers requires intentional steps:

- ✓ Lead with the why: Explain to children (and new believers) that Hallelujah is a declaration to God, not applause for humans.
- ✓ Model authentic worship: Let your personal Hallelujah demonstrate reverence, joy, and surrender. Children imitate hearts more than techniques.
- ✓ Create safe space for expression: Allow children and youth to worship freely, even if it is imperfect. Reverence trumps perfection.
- ✓ Incorporate Scripture: Pair every song with a story or verse that gives context, understanding, and depth.

**Closing Reflection**

Every Hallelujah we release today carries the potential to shape eternity. Worship leaders are not just serving congregations—they are training heirs to the throne of God. What we teach, model, and release in song and revelation will echo in the hearts of generations.

**A Real-life Example to Close:**

Jonah, a seasoned worship leader, spent years leading adult services. In his later years, he invested intentionally in a children's choir, teaching both songs and stories of God's power. Decades later, many of these children became worship leaders, pastors, and missionaries. Each of their Hallelujahs was shaped by the seeds sown under Jonah's faithful guidance.

Heaven rejoices not merely in what we sing, but in what we raise up to continue singing after us. Let every note, every declaration, and every Hallelujah we release today shape a generation who will also say Hallelujah in alignment, obedience, and eternal impact.

# CHAPTER 16
## *Your Personal Hallelujah Mandate*

Every revelation demands a response. After understanding the depth, authority, and eternal language of Hallelujah, the question is no longer *what does this word mean?* The question becomes *what will I do with it?* Revelation that remains admired but unapplied eventually fades. Revelation that is embraced becomes mandate.

Psalm 34:1 offers a startlingly bold confession from David: *"I will bless the Lord at all times; His praise shall continually be in my mouth."* David does not anchor this declaration to mood, victory, or ease. He roots it in will. *I will.* Hallelujah, at its most mature level, is not accidental worship—it is deliberate alignment. David's life proves that this was not poetic exaggeration. He praised while anointed but not crowned, celebrated while hunted, worshipped while repentant, and rejoiced while restored. His Hallelujah followed him through every version of himself.

This is the essence of a personal Hallelujah mandate. It is the decision that praise will no longer be occasional, reactive, or conditional. It will be continual—not because life is stable, but because God is faithful. A mandate is not a feeling; it is an assignment embraced.

The writer of Hebrews deepens this call when he urges believers to *"continually offer to God a sacrifice of praise—the fruit of lips that openly profess His name."* A sacrifice, by definition, costs something. Praise that costs nothing changes little. But praise offered when silence would be easier carries eternal weight. Hallelujah becomes a sacrifice when it is spoken despite fatigue, disappointment, or delay. That kind of praise is never ignored in heaven.

Throughout Scripture, God entrusts individuals with sounds that outlive their moments. Hannah's praise was born out of barrenness, yet it shaped prophetic history. Mary's Magnificat rose from uncertainty, yet it echoed redemption. These were not public performances; they were personal mandates fulfilled in surrender. Their Hallelujahs altered spiritual atmospheres because they were rooted in obedience.

In the New Testament, the early believers lived with this same awareness. Praise was not confined to gatherings; it was woven into daily life. They sang in prisons, rejoiced under persecution, and worshipped without platforms. Their Hallelujah was intentional. It was chosen. And because of that, it was contagious.

A beautiful story brings this mandate into modern clarity. Samuel was a quiet believer, faithful but hesitant. He admired worship leaders, envied their confidence, and assumed his contribution was minimal. Praise, to him, belonged to the expressive. One day, during a season of personal loss, he found himself alone, overwhelmed, and strangely compelled to speak gratitude aloud. His words were simple, imperfect, but sincere. In that moment, something shifted—not around him, but within him. He realized that Hallelujah was not about gifting; it was about obedience.

From that day forward, Samuel made a private commitment. He would not allow praise to be silenced by circumstance. He began speaking gratitude intentionally, praying Scripture aloud, and acknowledging God openly in daily conversation. Over time, others noticed—not his volume, but his peace. His life echoed heaven quietly, consistently. His Hallelujah became a witness.

This is the mandate extended to every reader of this book. Your praise must not be silenced. Not by disappointment. Not by familiarity. Not by fear of expression. Silence is rarely neutral; it often becomes agreement with discouragement. Hallelujah breaks that agreement.

Your Hallelujah must also be intentional. Worship that waits to be inspired will remain inconsistent. Worship that is chosen becomes stable. Intentional praise reshapes spiritual posture. It trains the heart to respond to God rather than react to life.

And ultimately, your life must echo heaven. Heaven does not struggle to praise. Heaven does not ration worship. Heaven does not wait for outcomes. Heaven worships because God is worthy. When a believer's life begins to reflect that reality—through words, actions, and attitudes—Hallelujah moves from lips to legacy.

This book does not end with a closing prayer because the assignment does not end here. Every day presents an altar. Every breath presents an opportunity. When you say Hallelujah, you are not filling space—you are releasing eternity into time.

Heaven understands that sound.

Now the question is simple, and unavoidable:

*Will your Hallelujah be heard?*

# APPENDIX
## *Stewarding the Sound:* A Worship Leader's Field Guide

### Stewarding the Sound: A Worship Leader's Field Guide

Worship leadership is more than talent—it is stewardship. The platform, the instruments, the voices, and even the emotions are all channels through which God's glory flows. But stewardship requires intentionality. Every worship leader must learn to cultivate the conditions for Hallelujah to carry authority, to protect unity, and to steward both hearts and sound.

### Preparing Spiritually Before a Service

The first responsibility of a worship leader is self-alignment. Public worship flows from private devotion. Moses consecrated the priests before they entered the tabernacle; David composed songs in the fields before leading armies in worship (1 Chronicles 15:16–28).

Consider the example of Reuben, a worship pastor who always arrived at the church hours before rehearsal. In those hours, he prayed, read Scripture, and aligned his heart with God's purposes for the service. He observed that rehearsals ran smoother, the team's focus sharpened, and congregational participation deepened. Spiritual preparation ensures that the Hallelujah released is not just technique, but authority.

### Reading the Room vs Following the Spirit

Modern worship often pressures leaders to react to the energy in the room. Yet heaven measures alignment, not crowd response. Psalm 33:3 calls for singing skillfully with a shout of joy—not for applause. Imagine Miriam, leading a youth service where the crowd seemed distracted. She felt an unction to pause and pray quietly with her team. Though the congregation initially murmured, the atmosphere shifted, and authentic engagement followed. Reading the room is helpful, but the ultimate guide is the Spirit. Following God's prompt may initially feel counterintuitive, but it always produces enduring impact.

### When to Linger, When to Move On

Leadership requires discernment: not every song or spontaneous moment should be prolonged. Ecclesiastes 3 reminds us that there is *"a time for everything."*

Consider Eliab, a worship leader who once extended a spontaneous Hallelujah for twenty minutes. Hearts were touched, but the message of the service was disrupted. Later, he learned to sense the Spirit's timing—lingering when heaven is present, moving on when the focus is complete. This ensures that every expression of praise carries maximum authority without creating confusion or fatigue.

### Handling Spontaneous Hallelujah Moments Without Chaos

True worship authority invites spontaneity, but chaos is not the mark of Heaven. Corporate worship requires structure within freedom.

Naomi led a midweek service where someone began a spontaneous chorus of praise. She had trained her team to respond in harmony—instrumentalists adjusted, vocalists complemented, and the congregation followed. The moment became one of profound unison, not disarray. Leadership in these moments preserves both freedom and order, allowing Hallelujah to move without friction.

**Protecting Unity on the Platform**

A worship leader must serve the team and the congregation, not personal ego. Paul's letters emphasize the body working together in love (1 Corinthians 12). Division on the platform disrupts authority.

Consider the story of Caleb and Miriam, co-leaders in a growing church. Caleb preferred contemporary arrangements, Miriam leaned toward liturgical hymns. Conflict began affecting rehearsals. By intentionally discussing vision, listening to one another, and submitting personal preferences for the good of the team, they protected unity. When the team is aligned, every Hallelujah released carries double authority: the blessing of God and the witness of harmony.

**The Steward's Heart**

Stewardship is the distinguishing factor between a talented musician and a worship leader who moves heaven. It is not perfection in skill or emotion—it is intentionality in every action. Stewardship asks:

- ✓ *Am I aligned with God before and during service?*
- ✓ *Am I attentive to the Spirit's guidance more than audience reaction?*

- ✓ *Am I leading my team in a way that multiplies authority rather than amplifying ego?*
- ✓ *Am I protecting the flow of worship, the hearts of the congregation, and the presence of God?*

**Closing Thought**

A worship leader is a steward of sound. Every note, every lyric, every spontaneous Hallelujah is an investment in eternity. Proper stewardship transforms moments into movements, platforms into altars, and songs into conduits of heaven.

When leaders embrace this, the sound they release will not only fill rooms—it will shift atmospheres, break chains, and release eternity.

# About the Author
## 'GERARD ASSEY'

Gerard Assey is a Graduate in Economics, a PGD in Management (HRD) and holds a Doctorate in Leadership. Gerard holds several International Qualifications in Sales, Debt Collection, Training & Teaching, and is a 'Fellow' of the prestigious 'Institute of Sales & Marketing Management'-UK, a Certified NLP Practitioner, a 'Certified Trainer', an 'Accredited Management Teacher-Behavioral Sciences', a 'Certified Competency Facilitator', a 'Certified Management Consultant'- (the International credentials of a professional management consultant, awarded in accordance with global standards of the ICMCI); and a Certification from the University of Michigan in 'Successful Negotiation: Essential Strategies and Skills'

He is also a Member of the 'National Association of Sales Professionals' backed with several years experience in varied industries, both in India and Overseas. He also holds an 'Etiquette Consultant' Certification from the USA (by Sue Fox, Author of Best Seller: 'Business Etiquette for Dummies'. She has trained some of the top celebrities' world over). He was also a recipient of a scholarship for extensive training in Japan on 'Corporate Management for India'.

Gerard Assey is 'Founder & Chief Corporate Trainer' of the Group: '**Citius, Altius, Fortius Unlimited**'- an organization that **celebrated 20 years of Glorious Service** in 2021, focusing on 3 Core Competencies:

**People. Performance. Profit**; in functional areas of Sales & Marketing, HR & Organizational Development, covering Recruitment, Training & Consultancy!

Having managed organizations with large Sales Forces in India & Overseas, his specialization cover extensive areas of Sales Training (All levels - Presentation, Negotiation, Key/ Strategic Accounts Management & Managerial Skills for all sectors), Bid Proposal/ Capture Planning/ Management Trainings, Retail Sales, Customer Service & Customer Retention Programs, Training for Prevention & Collection of Debt, Self & Personal Development Programs (Time Management, Teamwork & Team Building, Business Etiquette & Personal Grooming, Leadership & Managerial Skills, People Management Skills, Train-the-Trainer etc), including preparation of Custom-designed Business Manuals for Internal (HR, Induction, and Sales etc) & External use (Instruction, User Manuals).

Gerard has successfully conducted over 6495 Trainings & Workshops (as of Jan '26) all across India, Middle East, Africa, Europe & S.E. Asia. Besides public programs conducted regularly, both in India & Overseas, he has some of the top names as clients whom he services from Single Owners to large Public & Government undertakings, covering all sectors, for their in-house needs.

His website: www.CollectionSkills.com is the only one in this part of the world to be featured in the 'Collections & Credit Risk Magazine-USA' under 'Who's Who in Training' and ranks TOP, along with other websites listed below on most search engines.

**Gerard is author of 216 Books already (Jan 2026),** all the books being available on all online platforms and outlets as E-books and Paperbacks

**A few of our business related books:**

1. Bite-sized Bits on Commonsense Management
2. Heart to Heart on Life's Principles'
3. How to become a Successful Manager
4. The Sales Professionals' Master Workbook of S.Y.S.T.E.M.S
5. The Professional Business Email Etiquette Handbook & Guide
6. The Professional Business Video-Conferencing Etiquette Handbook & Guide
7. Professional Presentation Skills
8. Exceptional Customer Service
9. Professional Tele-Marketing Skills
10. Professional Debt Collection Skills
11. The G.R.E.A.T. Sales & Service Workbook
12. Sales Training Advantage for Results (*The Ultimate Sales Training Manual to enable you stand out as a S.T.A.R.*)
13. CEO Daily Planner & Organizer
14. The Sales Professionals' Master Daily Planner
15. The Professional Debt Collector's Master Daily Planner
16. My Daily Planner & Organizer
17. MY EMERGENCY INFORMATION RECORD (Family Emergency & Peace of Mind Planner)
18. The Ultimate Therapist & Counselors Planner and Organizer
19. Building an Ethical Workplace
20. Managing Relationships at Work
21. Managing Business Meetings Effectively
22. Effective Delegation Skills
23. Goal Setting for Success
24. B2B Selling by Email
25. Professional Business Etiquette & Grooming
26. Dining Etiquette & Table Manners
27. Effective Networking Skills
28. Grooming, Etiquette & Manners for Teens, Young Adults & Future Leaders
29. Inter-Personal Skills
30. Get Ready, Get Hired!
31. Selling in a Recession
32. Effective Receivables Management in an Economic Downturn!
33. Real Estate & Property Sales Training
34. Credit Sales & Accounts Receivable Management

35. Selling Skills for Real Estate & Property Advisors
36. Take G.R.E.A.T. C.A.R.E!
37. Spa, Salon & Health Club Selling Skills
38. Selling Travel, Holiday & MICE Services
39. Selling Skills for Spa's, Salons & Health Clubs
40. Retailing in Salons & Spas
41. Selling Holiday, Vacation, Tours & Packages
42. The Power of Sales Referrals
43. Selling Luxury
44. Technical Selling Skills
45. Financial Advisors Sales Training
46. Dealing with Burnout at Work Monopolize Your Markets
47. Selling to Affluent Customers
48. Growing up with Grace
49. Financial Selling Skills
50. *The Effective Manager's Guide: Key Skills to Thrive*
51. From Aspiring to Inspiring: A Guide for New Managers on the Rise
52. The Power of Focus
53. Selling with Integrity: Sell Like Jesus The Perfect Role Model!
54. 31 Habits of Champions: Your 31-Day Journey to Greatness
55. Rejecting Grasshopper Talk: From Grasshopper to Giant-Killer-*Defeating Giants Daily!*
56. Navigate the AI-Powered Future of Bid & Proposals: Up-Skill to Stay Relevant with Alternative Career Paths & Opportunities
57. Hiring Sales Winners
58. Present with Impact
59. Success Unlocked: *Breaking Free from Habits that Hold You Back*
60. Complaints to Cheers, Feedback to Gold: Mastering Complaints Management
61. Thriving Together: *Cultivating Diversity, Equity, and Inclusion*
62. Coaching Skills for Sales Managers
63. Soaring to Success in Business & Leadership: Swifter, Higher, Stronger!
64. From Classroom to Podium: A Student's Guide to Powerful Public Speaking & Presentation Skills
65. Developing Self-Discipline
66. The CEO's 31-Day Power Plan: Unlocking Success through Essential Traits

67. Credibility Matters
68. A Winning Attitude
69. Bid & Proposal Management Using AI
70. Sales Forecasting: A Practical & Proven Guide to Strategic Sales Forecasting
71. Elevate & Energize: *50 Dynamic & Fun Activities for Peak Workplace Morale*
72. 'Sales SOS! Sales on Fire! *30 Days to Conquer Chaos & the Nightmares of Success!'*
73. Mastering Sales Managerial Skills: *Building High-Performing Teams & Driving Exceptional Results*
74. Eagle-Eyed Leadership: Unleashing the Power of 31 Lessons from Eagles
75. The Ultimate Employee Training Guide: *Training Today, Leading Tomorrow*
76. Being More Accountable at Work
77. Creating a Culture of Continuous Improvement
78. Effective Questioning & Listening Skills
79. The Power of Value Selling
80. The Growth Mindset
81. Mastering Professional Help Desk Skills
82. The Power to Lead with Empathy
83. Being Prepared: The Key to Unlocking Success
84. Youthful Spark-Youth Energizers, Activities and Games-Igniting the Fun in Youth
85. Ignite your Motivation for Success
86. Elevate Your Executive Presence: *Your Roadmap to Executive Excellence*
87. Smart Decisions: *Mastering Problem Solving with Strategic Solutions for Business Success*
88. Strategic Planning: *Developing and Implementing Strategic Plans to Achieve Long-Term Business Goals*
89. The Power of Stay Interviews
90. Developing G.R.I.T.
91. Adaptability
92. Diagnosis- *A Key Skill for Leadership*
93. The Burnout-Proof Salesperson: *The Master Guide to Preventing Stress & Burnout-* Strategies for Thriving in Sales
94. Learning from Failure: *Keys to Success*
95. Customer Success Management
96. Overcoming the Killers of Motivation
97. The C-Suite Code: *Mastering Skills for Executive Excellence'*

98. Dealing with Difficult Customers
99. Unlocking Your Potential: Mastering the Top 20 Life Skills for a Brighter Future
100. Nurturing Tomorrow's Leaders: *Essential Soft Skills Every Child Must Learn*
101. Lively & Fun Party Games for Seniors & Elders
102. Role Playing for Sales Champions: From Practice to Performance
103. Fun and Exciting Party Games for Kids
104. Case Studies for Sales
105. Role-Playing for Unbeatable Customer Service
106. Case Studies in Customer Service
107. Case Studies in Winning Negotiations
108. Case Studies in Management & Leadership
109. Case Studies in Human Resources & Talent Management
110. CEO Success Blueprint: The Essential Toolkit for CEOs and C-Level Executives
111. The Salesperson's Self-Coaching Guide: *Master Your Own Self-Coaching Plan for Success*
112. Overcoming Procrastination: *Your Ultimate Guide to Stop Delaying and Start Living Your Best Life*
113. When True Colors Are Exposed: *The Journey to Unmasking Humanity*
114. Life-Changing Habits for Teens: Teen Success Blueprint for a Bright Future
115. Workplace Stress-Free: *Proven Strategies to Thrive at Work and Beyond*
116. Objection Overruled: *The Ultimate Guide to Turning 'No' into 'Yes'*
117. Building Strong Teams: *A Comprehensive Guide to Team Building*
118. Ethical & Moral Leadership in Business: *Eliminating Unethical Practices & Building a Culture of Trust & Integrity*
119. Rising Strong: Building Positive: High Self-Esteem for a Fulfilling Life-*A Practical Guide for Students, Employees, Leaders & Entrepreneurs*
120 The Cheerful Mindset: Cultivating a Joyful Outlook Everyday
121. Leading Through Crisis: Case Studies on Crisis Management
122. Selling Beyond the Algorithms

From the Ministry side, Gerard graduated in the very first batch of Charis Bible College-India & had for over 9 years served as a Part-time Faculty at Charis Bible College-Chennai (Andrew Wommack Ministries-Colorado, USA).
He also holds a Diploma in Worship (a subject closest to his heart) from the JSOW and is also a graduate of the Advanced Mentorship Program (AMP) and the Circle Of Ministerial Engagement (C.O.M.E.) of Prophet Jerome Fernando and a Spiritual Son of the Esteemed Prophet.
An accomplished author of several Secular & Christian Books, Gerard has been on the board of a few international organizations and boasts of being the SON of the MOST HIGH GOD: An ordinary guy following an extraordinary GOD!

**...And some of his most recent Christian Books being:**

1. A Bouquet of Praises for My KING
2. Christian Jokes for the Serious Religious' Folks!
3. Jesus Healed You!
4. Praise24Ever! (also in Tamil version)
5. The 5G Network of GOD
6. Building Faith over F.E.A.R- FACE EVERYTHING AND RISE with JESUS
7. Hebrew and Greek Praise and Worship Words
8. Godly Mothers' and Grandmothers' Bible Story time for Kids!
9. Miracles of Jesus in Pictures
10. Raise your Praise all 365 Days
11. Thanking GOD with an Attitude of Gratitude
12. Meditating on the Attributes of GOD
13. Puppet Scripts
14. Alcohol Ruins, JESUS Reforms, Renews & Restores!
15. Habakkuk 2:2 Christian Daily Journal, Planner & Organizer
16. ABC of GOD's Word for Handwriting Practice
17. Daily Bible Verse Handwriting Practice (Building Godly Character & Faith through Cursive Handwriting Practice!)
18. Guiding Light: Fun & Faith-Building Bible Activities for Children
19. Rejecting Grasshopper Talk: From Grasshopper to Giant-Killer-*Defeating Giants Daily!*
20. Teen Titans of Faith: *Building Courage, Determination & Christ-like-Esteem*
21. I AM Empowered: *Unleashing Divine Power with Positive Declarations*

22. Be A Solution Provider-*From Passion to Purpose*: *A Biblical Guide to Being the Answer to the World!*
23. Miracles of JESUS
24. Parables of Jesus for a Meaningful Life!
25. A Grateful Heart: Importance of Sharing Testimonies of GOD's Grace
26. Melodies of Worship to JESUS: 31 Songs of Praise & Worship From My Heart to HIS!
27. I AM SO BLESSED!
28. My Daily Cup of Energizer
29. 31 Leadership Lessons *from* Jesus- *The Supreme Leader*
30. Peace Amidst Storms: A Biblical Guide to Conquering S.T.R.E.S.S.
31. Rise Above: 20 Biblical Eagle Lessons for Life's Triumphs
32. Godly Goal Setting: *The FAITHFUL Blueprint for a Purpose-Driven Life*
33. The Profound Attributes of our Mighty GOD: Understanding the 10S's of the Almighty
34. Worship Now, Worship Forever: *A Journey from Earthly Praise to Eternal Glory*
35. Unceasing Praise & Worship: *365 Days to Worship the King*
36. The ROAR Within: *Living with Purpose and Authority through the Power of the Holy Spirit*
37. From Potential to Purpose: Unlocking and Multiplying Your Talents & Gifts for Kingdom Impact
38. Songs from the Heart: *Worshipping GOD in Your Own Tune & Melody*
39. Awakening Praise & Worship: Hebrew & Greek Words to Raise Your Praise
40. Sing a NEW Song to the LORD Everyday: *Daily Devotions of Praise & Worship to Lift Your Heart & Glorify HIS Name*
41. *The* A.R.O.M.A. of True Worship: *Creating Worship That Delights God*
42. Becoming A Kingdom Champion: *Embracing God's Call for a Life of Purpose & Victory*
43. The Busy Businessman's Daily Devotional: 366 Crisp Truths to Start Your Day Strong
44. The Teacher's Heart: *Daily Devotions for Educators*
45. Anchored! *A 31-Day Devotional for Students Facing Life's Challenges*
46. Suddenly! Unlocking Unorthodox Breakthroughs through Unusual Worship
47. Overcoming Adversity: *Lessons from the Bible for Modern*

*Challenges*

48. LORD, Don't do it without me
49. Kingdom Leadership: *Biblical Principles for Modern Leaders*
50. Heartprints of God- *Growing God's Way:* Daily Devotions for Kids to Shine Bright
51. Send Judah First: Let your Praises Go up First to See the Mighty Move of GOD
52. DIVINE MOMENTS: *Recognizing, Embracing, Preparing, and Walking into Life-Changing Encounters with God*
53. Be a Builder in the Kingdom: *The C.E.M.E.N.T. Guide to Creating a Lasting Legacy*
54. Unshakable: *Pillars of Godly Womanhood* (Pillars of Faith That Changed History)
55. Lead Like a Shepherd: *14 Essential Traits for Pastoral Excellence*
56. The Worship Leader's Arsenal: *Powerful Exhortations to Ignite Thanksgiving, Praise & Worship*
57. Women of UnShakable Faith: *31-Day Devotional for Strength, Purpose & Influence*
58. Called to Teach: *A Complete 10-Week Training Guide for Impactful VBS Teachers*
59. Strumming for the KING: Cowboy Songs of Faith & Fire
60. The Ultimate Youth Camp Playbook: *50 Bible-Centered Indoor Games to Engage, Equip, and Empower Teens*
61. Glad in HIS Presence: *David's Revelation of GOD's Love & Mercy*
62. The Spirit Behind the Sound: *52 Devotionals for Worship Teams*
63. THE COWBOY'S COMPASS: *Riding the Trail of Faith with Grit & Grace*
64. Worship as My Weapon: *Living Victoriously through the Power of Praise*
65. A Worshipper Always Wins*: Living a Life of Victorious Worship*
66. Worship That Leads to the Throne: *Practical Strategies for Worship Leaders to Inspire Their Team & Usher People into God's Presence*
67. Worship as Warfare: *Conquering through the Sound of Surrender*
68. Watchmen on the Walls: *A 31-Day Devotional for Worship Teams*
69. KINGDOM BUSINESS: *52 Biblical Principles for GODLY*

*Leadership & Wise Decisions*

70. From Evening to Morning: *Rediscovering GOD's Sacred Hours*
71. Waves of Glory: *Worship through Dance, Flags, Staff & Sound*
72. WORSHIP TEAM BUILDER: *Guiding Your Team from Formation to Fruitfulness*
73. The Worship Leader's Master Training Manual
74. Skits for the King: Children's Plays for Every Church Occasion
75. Unbreakable: Building Strong Marriages and Families God's Way *(From Vows to Victory)*
76. Songs for my King: *A 31-Day Journey of Praise*
77. Building Powerful Children: *Raising a Generation That Will Shape the Future for God*
78. Character Before Chords: *The Heart of the True Worshipper*
79. 365 Days Before His Throne: A Worshipper's Daily Declarations
80. Broken to Built: *How GOD Restores Lives, Heals Hearts & Uses Broken People for HIS Glory*
81. Fear Did Not Come from God: *Discerning the Source, Dismantling the Stronghold & Walking in Power, Love & a Sound Mind*
82. THE GOD OF BEGINNINGS: *Positioning Your Life for What God Is About to Start*
83. HEALED ALREADY: IT IS FINISHED! Receiving What the Cross Has Completed!
84. A.D.D.E.D. Y.E.A.R.S. When God Overrules the Clock, the Diagnosis, and the Final Word
85. HALLELUJAH -The Sound That Heaven Understands *(Building a Life of Pure Praise)*

Besides regularly contributing to business & trade journals, including international ones such as the 'Creative Training Techniques' and the 'Sales News' of the U.S.A, He is also a member of several prestigious bodies & trade associations, having participated in many Conferences & Workshops in India & Overseas.

Prior to his last assignment of leading & managing a

large MNC as head, Gerard had a 3-year stint in the Middle East as a Consultant with a leading British Consultancy Firm.

As the past 'Official Country Representative' for the International Business Award- 'THE STEVIES'-(the business world's own Oscar) for about 4 years- he ensured a few Indian companies that qualify for the same every year!

Gerard can be contacted at:

Email: training@Sales-Training.in,training@CollectionSkills.com
Websites:

www.Sales-Training.in
www.EtiquetteWorks.in
www.CollectionSkills.com
www.RetailSalesTraining.in
www.SalesTrainingIndia.com
www.ManualPreparation.com
www.TrainingWithPuppets.com
www.FirstContactAcademy.com
www.SalesAndMarketingRecruiter.com

www.ingramcontent.com/pod-product-compliance
Ingram Content Group UK Ltd.
Pitfield, Milton Keynes, MK11 3LW, UK
UKHW021341190726
13845UKWH00027B/657

9 788199 513426